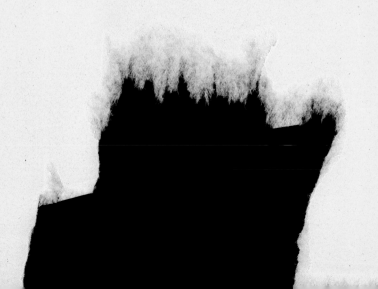

TO FRANCES E. WILLARD

Bureau of Engraving and Printing.

Statue

of

Miss Frances E. Willard

Erected in Statuary Hall of the
Capitol Building at Washington

Proceedings in the Senate and House
of Representatives on the Occasion of
the Reception and Acceptance of the
Statue from the State of Illinois : : :

Compiled under the direction of the
Joint Committee on Printing

Washington
Government Printing Office
1905

CONCURRENT RESOLUTION.

Resolved by the Senate (the House of Representatives concurring), That there be printed and bound of the proceedings in Congress upon the acceptance of the statue of the late Frances E. Willard, presented by the State of Illinois, sixteen thousand five hundred copies, of which five thousand shall be for the use of the Senate, ten thousand for the use of the House of Representatives, and the remaining one thousand five hundred shall be for the use and distribution by the governor of the State of Illinois; and the Secretary of the Treasury is hereby directed to have printed an engraving of said statue to accompany said proceedings, said engraving to be paid for out of the appropriation for the Bureau of Engraving and Printing.

Passed the Senate February 23, 1905.

Passed the House of Representatives March 3, 1905.

2

Table of Contents

Acceptance

of the

Statue of Miss Frances E. Willard

❧

Proceedings in the Senate

❧

The PRESIDING OFFICER (Mr. Perkins) laid before the Senate a communication from the governor of the State of Illinois, requesting that a date be fixed for the acceptance by Congress of the statue of FRANCES E. WILLARD; which was referred to the Committee on the Library, and ordered to be printed.

STATUE OF FRANCES E. WILLARD.

Mr. WETMORE. I am directed by the Committee on the Library, to whom was referred yesterday the letter of the governor of Illinois in regard to the acceptance by Congress, on a date to be fixed, of the statue of FRANCES E. WILLARD, to report it back, and I ask that it may lie on the table.

The PRESIDING OFFICER. The Committee on the Library will be discharged from the further consideration of the communication of the governor of Illinois.

Mr. CULLOM. I ask that the letter be laid on the table for the time being, I shall call it up at some future day.

5

The Presiding Officer. The request of the senior Senator from Illinois will be agreed to, and the communication will lie on the table subject to his call.

JANUARY 17, 1905.

STATUE OF FRANCES E. WILLARD.

Mr. Cullom. I offer a resolution and ask for its immediate consideration. Before the resolution is read, I ask that a letter addressed to the President of the Senate by the governor of my State may be read.

The President pro tempore. If there is no objection, the letter will be read. The Chair hears none.

The Secretary read as follows:

STATE OF ILLINOIS, EXECUTIVE DEPARTMENT,
Springfield, January 10, 1905.

DEAR SIR: Governor Deneen is in receipt of a letter from the chairman of the Illinois board of commissioners for the FRANCES E. WILLARD statue, informing him that the sculptor, Helen Farnsworth Mears, reports that the model will reach Washington, D. C., on February 11. The commissioners express the desire that Governor Deneen advise the Senate of the United States and House of Representatives of the completion of the statue, in order that a date may be immediately fixed for its acceptance by Congress. I am directed by Governor Deneen to communicate this fact to you for your information and such action as Congress may see fit to take.

Yours, truly,

J. WHITTAKER,
Secretary.

Hon. WILLIAM P. FRYE,
President United States Senate, Washington, D. C.

The President pro tempore. The resolution submitted by the Senator from Illinois will be read.

The resolution was read, considered by unanimous consent, and agreed to, as follows:

Resolved, That the exercises appropriate to the reception and acceptance from the State of Illinois of the statue of FRANCES E. WILLARD, erected in Statuary Hall, in the Capitol, be made the special order for Friday, February 17, at 3 o'clock.

Memorial Exercises

Friday, February 17, 1905.

The Chaplain, Rev. Edward E. Hale, said:

The Congress has devoted a part of to-day to memorial exercises in honor of Miss FRANCES E. WILLARD, the distinguished philanthropist, to whom the nation is so largely indebted. Let me read for our Scripture lesson such verses from King Lemuel's description as are appropriate to this distinguished woman:

A virtuous woman who can find? for her price is far above rubies. She doeth good and not evil all the days of her life. She girdeth her loins with strength and maketh strong her arms. She spreadeth out her hand to the poor. Strength and dignity are her clothing. She openeth her mouth with wisdom and the law of kindness is on her tongue. A woman that feareth the Lord, she shall be praised. Give her of the fruit of her hand and let her works praise her in the gates.

Let us pray.

Father Almighty, we remember what Thou hast given this nation in sending such an apostle of Thy word; of Thine own righteousness. She taught this people that the wisdom from above is first pure, and she showed them how to add to their purity, peace, and gentleness by those efforts by which men shall work with God for the coming of His kingdom.

Father, we remember her. We preserve the memorials of such a life. But it is not for the past; it is for the future that we pray, that the people of this land may know what it is to be pure in body, pure in heart, pure in soul; that they may offer to Thee the living sacrifice; that men and women may know that they are the living temples of the living God.

Be with us in the services of to-day. Be with this nation—North, South, East, West—in the schoolroom, in the church, and in daily duty, as men and women seek to draw nearer to God, and yet nearer—yes, Father, even though it were a cross that raiseth us—that we may come nearer to Thee. We ask it in His name.

Our Father who art in Heaven, Hallowed be Thy name. Thy kingdom come. Thy will be done on earth as it is done in Heaven. Give us this day our daily bread. And forgive us our trespasses as we forgive those who trespass against us. And lead us not into temptation, but deliver us from evil: For Thine is the kingdom, and the power, and the glory, forever. Amen.

STATUE OF FRANCES E. WILLARD.

Mr. Cullom. Mr. President, the exercises for to-day are indicated in the following resolution:

Resolved, That the exercises appropriate to the reception and acceptance from the State of Illinois of the statue of Frances E. Willard, erected in Statuary Hall, in the Capitol, be made the special order for Friday, February 17, at 3 o'clock.

When the letter came from the State of Illinois, signed by the secretary of the governor of that State, it did not fully comply with the existing rule. The governor of the State was suddenly called away by the severe and sudden illness of his daughter, and in his absence the secretary sent the letter to the Senate. The governor of the State therefore desires that the following telegram may be read, so that it may go upon the record and be a part of the proceedings.

The PRESIDENT pro tempore. The Secretary will read as requested.

The Secretary read as follows:

[Telegram.]

SPRINGFIELD, ILL., *February 16, 1905.*

Hon. SHELBY M. CULLOM,
　　United States Senator, Washington, D. C.:
　Will you kindly submit the following to the Senate and House of Representatives?

CHAS. S. DENEEN.

STATE OF ILLINOIS, EXECUTIVE DEPARTMENT,
　　　　　　Springfield, February 16, 1905.
To the Senate and House of Representatives
　　　of the United States, Washington, D. C.

GENTLEMEN : By authority of the act of the general assembly of Illinois, the governor of Illinois heretofore appointed Anna A. Gordon, Mary E. Metzgar, John J. Mitchell, W. R. Jewell, and Mrs. S. M. D. Fry to constitute a commission to procure a statue of FRANCES E. WILLARD for erection in Statuary Hall, in the Capitol at Washington, D. C. I am informed by the commissioners that the statue was made by Helen F. Mears, of New York City; that it is completed and has been placed in position, and is now ready to be presented to Congress. I have been further informed by Miss Anna A. Gordon, chairman of the commissioners, that a resolution is to be presented accepting said statue. As governor of the State of Illinois, therefore, I have the honor to present to the Government of the United States the statue hereinbefore referred to.

　　Very respectfully,

CHAS. S. DENEEN,
Governor of Illinois.

Mr. CULLOM. I submit the resolutions I send to the desk.

The PRESIDENT pro tempore. The Senator from Illinois presents resolutions, which will be read by the Secretary.

The Secretary read the resolutions, and the Senate proceeded to their consideration, as follows:

Resolved by the Senate (*the House of Representatives concurring*), That the statue of FRANCES E. WILLARD, presented by the State of Illinois, to be placed in Statuary Hall, be accepted by the United States, and that the thanks of Congress be tendered the State for the statue of one of the most eminent women of the United States.

Resolved, That a copy of these resolutions, duly authenticated, be transmitted to the governor of the State of Illinois.

Address of Mr. Cullom, of Illinois

Mr. PRESIDENT: The State of Illinois presents to the United States the statue of a great woman, whose name is familiar wherever the English language is spoken.

The Senate has frequently suspended its ordinary business to pay tribute to the memory of eminent statesmen who have passed away. During the present session we have heard eloquent eulogies on the lives of two distinguished men—George Frisbie Hoar, of Massachusetts, and John J. Ingalls, of Kansas. For the first time in the history of the Senate a day has been set apart that we may talk of a woman.

More than forty years ago, after the new Hall of the House of Representatives was constructed, it became a problem to know to what use the old hall, in which the greatest men in the early days of the Republic had occupied seats, should be dedicated.

Senator Morrill first made the suggestion, which was afterwards enacted into a law, that the old Hall be set apart as a national statuary hall, and that each State be invited to provide two statues of its illustrious citizens to be placed therein.

Twenty States have responded, each State naturally selecting two of its most illustrious citizens. There are statues of Robert Winthrop and Daniel Webster, of Massachusetts; Roger Williams, of Rhode Island; George Clinton and Robert Fulton, of New York; Ethan Allen, of Vermont; Roger Sherman, of Connecticut; Oliver P. Morton, of Indiana; James A. Garfield, of Ohio; and many other distinguished men, whom their respective States deemed worthy of so high an honor.

Illinois has been the home of many eminent men. Cook and Pope, in the early history of the State; Lincoln, than whom no nobler man ever lived; Grant, one of the most renowned generals of the age; Douglas, a noted statesman, whose career in the Senate was marked by wonderful power; Trumbull, who for many years occupied a seat in this Chamber, and as chairman of the Committee on the Judiciary, was recognized as a profound lawyer and statesman; Davis, who was an honored member of the Supreme Court of the United States, and was subsequently President pro tempore of this body; Logan, an able Member of the House of Representatives, the greatest volunteer soldier of the civil war, and for years a leading Senator in this Chamber; and many other great names whose deeds have illumined the pages of our nation's history; yet, with so large a number of splendid men from whom to make a selection, the State of Illinois selected a woman thus so signally to honor.

Mr. President, Miss WILLARD was a worthy representative of her sex, known to the world for her devotion to the cause of temperance and for her efforts in the interest of the human race.

She .had a wonderful career. Beginning in poverty, struggling with adverse conditions, with courage and faith in the right she overcame all obstacles in her pathway, and became one of the foremost women of her time.

The story of her life is inspiring to her sex and uplifting to humanity. She was born in Churchville, N. Y., September 28, 1839, being a descendant of the well-known WILLARD family of Massachusetts, the first of whom settled in the New World in 1634, and was one of the founders of Concord, later the home of many famous men of letters.

The Willards were noted men and women of New England before and during the Revolution. Her parents were brave, honest, intellectual, strong-minded, patriotic Christian people.

They were among that band of pioneers who left New England about 1840 to seek their fortunes in the West. In 1846 the Willard family located near Janesville, Wis., on the banks of the beautiful Rock River. Here, on her father's farm, the early life of Miss WILLARD was spent.

Even as a child she is said to have been eager to grapple with principles and philosophies, and from childhood she seemed to feel that she was destined to perform an important work in the world.

Long years afterwards she speaks thus of her early life, spent at Forest Home, on the banks of Rock River:

It was a beautiful childhood. I do not know how it could have been more beautiful, or how there could have been a truer beginning of many things. To me it has often seemed as if those earlier years were seed to all my after good.

Long years have left their writing on my brow, but yet the freshness and the dew-fed beam of those young mornings are about me now. Wherever I may dwell no place can be so dear, so completely embalmed in my heart, so truly the best beloved to me, as Forest Home.

Miss WILLARD attended the Northwestern Female College, at Evanston, Ill., a woman's college of high grade in the West, from which she was graduated with honor. After teaching at several institutions of learning she completed her education by two years of travel and study abroad.

In 1871 she became president of the Evanston College for Ladies, the first female college entirely under the control and direction of women, of which a woman was president and women constituted the board of trustees. This college was later made the woman's department of the Northwestern University, one of the leading institutions of learning of the West, and Miss WILLARD became dean and professor of æsthetics.

In 1874 she resigned her connection with the Northwestern University. Some years afterwards, when the famous evangelist, Moody, invited her to become associated with him as a coadjutor in his work, and inquired why she left the North-western University, she gave this characteristic answer:

Doctor Fowler, the president of the institution, has the will of Napoleon. I have the will of Queen Elizabeth. When an immovable meets an inde-structible object something has to give way.

Mr. Moody made no further inquiry.

On her resignation from the Northwestern University Miss WILLARD had many flattering offers to continue in the educa-tional world, where she would in a few years have become the foremost woman educator in the United States, but she declined them all.

In 1873 a great woman's Christian crusade on temperance was commenced, originating in Ohio. Miss WILLARD was early attracted toward the temperance movement. She saw in it an opportunity to perform a great service in the interest of the human race. With alacrity she accepted the invitation to become president of the Illinois Woman's Christian Temper-ance Union, and, abandoning a brilliant educational career, in 1874 she entered on what was to be her last work. From that time until her death, for more than a quarter of a century, she devoted her splendid energies to the temperance cause and other reforms.

The Illinois Woman's Christian Temperance Union, when Miss WILLARD was elected as its president, was a small band of women, the outgrowth of the women's crusade. She received no salary, but gave her whole time to the work, addressing large noonday meetings daily in the worst districts of Chicago, practically living on the charity of her friends.

In 1879 she was elected president of the National Woman's Christian Temperance Union, and in that position her splendid executive ability and faculty for organization had full sway. She traveled over this country constantly, talking in behalf of her white ribbon cause in every town and city in the United States having a population of 10,000 or more. In 1883 she projected the World's Woman's Christian Temperance Union, of which she later became president. Under her leadership the temperance crusade spread as if by magic throughout the United States.

Not content with what she had accomplished here at home, on several occasions she visited England and assisted the temperance movement, where she addressed immense audiences in different parts of that country.

Miss WILLARD was not only an advocate of temperance, but of all other beneficial, progressive reforms—purity in politics, equal rights for women, and, as a means to secure political reform, woman suffrage. She believed ''that there is such a power in the influence of women as, if it were exerted right, would shake the kingdom to the center.''

She was recognized as an able public speaker, perhaps the greatest woman speaker in the country. She had a rare gift of eloquence and magnetism which drew thousands into the temperance ranks. During her years of active life she probably addressed a larger number of public audiences than any man or woman of her time.

What did the Woman's Christian Temperance Union accomplish under the leadership of FRANCES E. WILLARD? She lived to see it grow from a small, struggling organization with which she was connected in 1879 to a world-wide movement, the most splendid organization of women that ever existed, numbering in the United States more than 300,000, with a following of half a million. In 10,000 towns and cities local unions were established. The Loyal Temperance Legion was formed, composed of children, with a membership of over 250,000. Temperance instruction was provided in the schools and Sunday schools to more than 16,000,000 children. Tens of thousands of men were induced to sign the total-abstinence pledge. It circulated millions of pages of temperance literature, and it has gone far to secure equality of treatment of women. It appealed for happy homes—the source of good society and good government—home protection; it appealed to the mothers to save the boys for their country, and it marshaled every moral force to the support of its principles.

Miss WILLARD, notwithstanding her busy life and her varied duties as leader of this world-wide organization, found time to write many books. She was a woman of rare literary attainments, and some of her books have been circulated throughout the world and have been translated into several languages.

She was ambitious, but hers was a noble ambition. She says in her autobiography:

I have been called ambitious, and so I am, if to have had from childhood the sense of being born to a fate is an element of ambition. For I never knew what it was to aspire and not to believe myself capable of heroism. I always wanted to react upon the world about me to my utmost ounce of power, to be widely known, loved, and believed in—the more widely the better. Every life has its master passion; this has been mine. Very few things waken my contempt, but this couplet in the hymn book did:

> Make me little and unknown,
> Loved and prized by God alone.

Its supreme absurdity angered rather than amused me, for who could be "loved and prized" by the Great Spirit and yet despised by the lesser spirits made in his image? Who could deliberately desire to be "little and unknown," of small value and narrow circle in a world so hungry for help and strength and uplift, yet beloved and prized by God? No. I wanted to be now and in all worlds my very utmost. I fully purposed to be one whom the multitudes would love, lean on, and bless. Lying on the prairie grass, and lifting my hands toward the sky, I used to say in my inmost spirit, "What is it that I am to be, O God?" I did not wish to climb by others' overthrow, and I laid no schemes to undermine them, but I meant that the evolution of my own powers should do for me all that it would. I felt that a woman owed it to all other women to live as bravely, as helpfully, and as grandly as she could, and to let the world know it.

If ever the ambition of any man or woman was gratified, this ambition of Miss WILLARD was, and to the fullest extent. She did live bravely, helpfully, and grandly, and at the time of her death she was one of the most beloved women of America.

Mr. President, I esteem it an honor to have known personally FRANCES E. WILLARD during the greater part of her active life. I knew from personal knowledge of the work in which she was engaged, and I witnessed with pleasure the wonderful success which attended her efforts. She was a reformer, but she never shared the usual unpopularity of reformers, and her advocacy of reform in temperance never made her offensive to any class of people. Notwithstanding her public life, she was nevertheless a real woman, with that degree of sincerity and modesty that commanded the utmost respect from all with whom she came in contact.

Mr. President, I am proud that the State of Illinois was the home of FRANCES E. WILLARD.

Seven years ago to-morrow, the 18th of February, 1898, the sad news announced that she was no more. It seemed that the world stopped to mourn. No man or woman of her time received such splendid eulogy, not only from those engaged in her cause, not only from those who believed in her creed, but from the best representatives of all classes and all religions.

In the public press we saw such comments as these:

Her services to mankind were inestimable.

Her life was a power, not only for temperance and purity and right living of every kind, but for love and fellowship and brotherhood the world over.

The world will sorrow that such a great power for good has been taken away.

No history of hero worship would be complete without her wondrous story.

To-day the hushed voices and moistened eyes of thousands upon thousands of men and women throughout the world testify to the universal impression Miss WILLARD left upon her time.

17046—05——2

Her friend, Lady Henry Somerset, the temperance leader of Great Britain, said:

I believe that long after the temperance reform has become a matter of past history, long after the woman question has brought about the equality of men and women—political, social, and financial—the name of FRANCES E. WILLARD will be remembered not only as one who led a great movement, but as one who gave her life, her talent, her enthusiasm, to make the world wider for women and better for humanity. Such a record will be associated with no particular form of philanthropy, but will stand among the landmarks of the ages that point the progress of the world along all the upward way.

Illinois especially mourned the death of Miss WILLARD. It was in Illinois, in the vicinity of Chicago, that she commenced her great work and had lived for more than forty years, and it was to Illinois that her remains were brought, and it was there that the most touching tributes of respect were paid to her. Her body lay in state at Willard Hall, in the Women's Temple, in Chicago, where it was viewed by more than 20,000 people, composed of all classes, the rich and the poor, equally anxious to look for the last time on the face of the woman whose teachings had done so much for the world. The last services were held at Evanston, where great throngs of people assembled, and she was finally laid to rest at Rose Hill Cemetery, February 24, 1898.

The world has been better because FRANCES E. WILLARD lived. She devoted her life unselfishly to the cause of humanity, and she brought sobriety into the homes of untold thousands; and at her death she left an organization that has been and will continue to be a great potent factor for good in the world.

Mr. President, the State of Illinois, in presenting the statue to the United States, to be placed in Statuary Hall among the figures of the greatest men that have lived in the United States, has honored itself, has justly honored a great woman, and has paid a tribute to all American womanhood.

[Manifestations of applause in the galleries.]

Address of Mr. Beveridge, of Indiana

Mr. PRESIDENT: From the beginning woman has personified the world's ideals. When history began its record it found her already the chosen bride of Art. All things that minister to mankind's good have, from the very first, by the general judgment, been made feminine—the ships that bear us through storm to port; the seasons that bring variety, surcease of toil, and life's renewal; the earth itself, which, through all time and in all speech, has been the universal mother. The Graces were women, and the Muses, too. Always her influence has glorified the world, until her beatitude becomes divine in Mary, mother of God.

Mark how the noblest conceptions of the human mind have always been presented in form of woman. Take Liberty; take Justice; take all the holy aspirations, all the sacred realities! Each glorious ideal has, to the common thought, been feminine. The sculptors of the olden time made every immortal idea a daughter of the gods. Even Wisdom was a woman in the early concept of the race, and that unknown genius of the youthful world wrought Triumph itself into woman's form in that masterpiece of all ages—The Winged Victory. Over the lives and destinies of men the ancients placed Clotho, Lachesis, and Atropos forever spinning, twisting, severing the strands of human fate.

In the literature of all time woman has been Mercy's messenger, handmaid of tenderness, creator and preserver of human happiness. Name Shakespeare—Miranda, and Imo-

gene, Rosalind, Perdita, and Cordelia appear; name Burns—
the prayer "To Mary in Heaven" gives to the general
heart that touch of nature which makes the whole world
kin; name the Book of Books—Rachel and the women of
the Bible in beauty walk before us, and in the words of
Ruth we hear the ultimate formula of woman's eternal fidelity
and faith.

And so we see that through all time woman has typified
the true, the beautiful, and the good on earth. And now
Illinois, near the very heart of the world's great Republic
and at the dawn of the twentieth century, chooses woman
herself as the ideal of that Commonwealth and of this period;
for the character of FRANCES E. WILLARD is womanhood's
apotheosis.

And she was American. She was the child of our
American prairies, daughter of an American home. And so
she had strength and gentleness, simplicity and vision. Not
from the complex lives that wealth and luxury force upon
their unfortunate children; not from the sharpening and
hardening process of the city's social and business grind;
not from any of civilization's artificialities, come those whom
God appoints to lead mankind toward the light.

Moses dwelt alone on the summit of mystery and human
solitude. The Master abode in the wilderness, and there the
power descended on Him with which He put aside the
tempter. In the forests the father of our country learned
liberty's lessons from Nature, liberty's mother; and from the
valleys and the heights the fields and pouring streams got
understanding of the possibilities of this land, a knowledge
of its uses, a perception of its people's destiny. We can not
imagine Abraham Lincoln coming to us from a palace. No!
We can understand him only as he really was—man of the

people and the soil, thinking with the people's mind the grand and simple truths, feeling with the people's heart an infinite compassion for and fellowship with all the race.

And so, Mr. President, all the saints and heroes of this world have come, fresh and strong from the source of things, by abuses unspoiled and unweakened by false refinements. And so came FRANCES E. WILLARD, the American woman. The wide, free fields were the playgrounds of her childhood. The great primeval woods impressed her unfolding soul with their vast and vital calmness. Association with her neighbors was scant and difficult; and home meant to her all that the poets have sung of it, and more. It was a refuge and a shrine, a dwelling and a place of joy, a spot where peace and love and safety and all unselfishness reigned with a sovereignty unchallenged. And so this child of our forests and our plains, this daughter of that finest of civilization's advance guard— the American pioneers—early received into her very soul that conception of the home to which, as the apostle of universal womanhood, her whole life was dedicated.

To make the homes of the millions pure, to render sweet and strong those human relations which constitute the family—this was her mission and her work. And there can not be a wiser method of mankind's upliftment than this, no better way to make a nation noble and enduring; for the hearthstone is the foundation whereon the state is built. The family is the social and natural unit. Spencer wrote learnedly of "the individual aids the state;" but he wrote words merely. The individual is not the important factor in nature or the nation. Nature destroys the individual. Nature cares only for the pair; knows in some form nothing but the family. And so by the deep reasoning of nature itself FRANCES WILLARD'S work was justified.

But hers was no philosopher's creed.   She got her inspiration from a higher source than human thinking.   In her life's work we see restored to earth that faith which, whenever man has let it work its miracle, has wrought victory here and immortality hereafter.   Such was the faith of Joan, the inspired maid of France; such that of Columbus, sailing westward through the dark; such the exalted belief of those good missionaries who first invaded our American wildernesses to light with their own lives on civilization's altar the sacred fire that never dies.   The story of FRANCES E. WILLARD's faith in the conquest of evil by the good seems incredible to us who demand a map of all our future before we take a step.

For FRANCES E. WILLARD knew no questioning.   The Master's message was at once her guaranty and her command.   The Bible was to her, in very truth, divine.   What immeasurable and increasing influence that one book has wielded over the minds of men and the destiny of the world!   If it be the word of God, as we profoundly believe, surely it comes to human ears with all the dignity and peace and power that His word should command.   If it be the word of man, then even the doubter must admit that the ancient Hebrews had miraculous skill to cast a spell across millenniums which, strengthening with the years, spreads wider to-day than ever and embraces the future as far as even the eye of imagination can behold.   Not all invention or all statesmanship or all of literature have so touched and bettered human life as this one book.   And it was the Bible that gave FRANCES E. WILLARD her mission, her strength, her hope, her argument, and her inspiration.

Thus prepared and thus equipped she went out into the world and to her work.   No method can measure what she did.   The half million of women whom she brought into organized cooperation in the Woman's Christian Temperance Union is but a suggestion of the real results of her activities. Indeed, the highest benefits her life bestowed were as intangible as air and as full of life. She made purer the moral atmosphere of a continent—almost of a world. She rendered the life of a nation cleaner, the mind of a people saner. Millions of homes to-day are happier for her; millions of wives and mothers bless her; and countless children have grown into strong, upright, and beautiful maturity who, but for the work of FRANCES E. WILLARD, might have been forever soiled and weakened.

The mother of all mothers, the sister of all wives, to every child a lover, FRANCES E. WILLARD sacrificed her own life to the happiness of her sisters. For after all, she knew that with all her gifts and all the halo of her God-sent mission, nevertheless the humblest mother was yet greater far than she. But it was needful that she should so consecrate her strength and length of years. For how shall the service of utter unselfishness be achieved save in the utter sacrifice of self? So FRANCES E. WILLARD gave up her life and all the rights and glories of it that all of her sisters might lead fuller, richer, happier, sweeter lives themselves.

So, Mr. President, by placing her statue in the hall of our national immortals, a great Commonwealth to-day forever commemorates the services of this American woman to all humanity. And the Representatives of the American people— the greatest people in this world—in Congress formally assembled to-day are paying tribute to the little frontier American maid who heard and heeded the voices that came to her from the unseen world, and, obeying their counsels, became the first woman of the nineteenth century, the most beloved character of her time, and, under God, a benefactress of her race. [Applause in the galleries.]

Address of Mr. Hopkins, of Illinois

Mr. PRESIDENT: When the late Senator Morrill, of Vermont, proposed to dedicate the old Hall of the House of Representatives as a national Statuary Hall for the purpose of authorizing each of the States of the Union to place therein statues of deceased persons who had been citizens of such State and illustrious for their historic renown or for distinguished civic or military service, he little dreamed that the great State of Illinois in complying with that statute would select for one of her citizens a woman in the person of FRANCES E. WILLARD.

She was then a young woman. Her great future had hardly opened before her. She little dreamed at that period of her life that she would attain that civic distinction or historic renown that would warrant Illinois in selecting her as one of her representatives in Statuary Hall, or that Illinois would honor herself by passing over so many of her distinguished sons and select her as one of her representatives.

The years that have come and gone since the late Senator Morrill caused that law to be placed upon the statute books of our country saw Miss WILLARD advance step by step from the most humble beginnings until her fame became not only national but world-wide. Her services to her sex and humanity extended to every part of the civilized world, and when death claimed her, and her noble spirit passed into immortality, an enlightened and patriotic legislature of the State of Illinois selected her as worthy of a place in Statuary

Hall, dedicated by the several States to the most eminent and distinguished of all their sons.

The affection and regard in which the memory of Miss WILLARD is held by the people of Illinois, and the honor so worthily bestowed upon her in the proceedings of this day, will be better appreciated by the general public when we call to mind the names and number of distinguished men whom the legislators of Illinois might have chosen for this especial honor.

No State has been more fortunate than Illinois in this re-gard. Lincoln, Douglas, Bissell, Baker, Browning, Trumbull, Yates, Oglesby, Davis, Stephen T. Logan, Grant, John A. Logan, John M. Palmer, Gen. John A. McClernand, to say nothing of such men as Governor Coles, John A. Cook, Ninian Edwards, and Sidney Breese, present a list of brilliant and dis-tinguished men whose abilities and achievements not only enrich the pages of the history of Illinois, but of the nation as well.

Lincoln, who was born in a log hut on the outskirts of civili-zation in the State of Kentucky, came to Illinois in his boy-hood, and on the broad and fertile prairies of that State devel-oped those qualities of head and heart that made him the fore-most man of his generation and placed his name among the immortals.

Douglas, although born in New England, when a mere boy sought his fortunes in the West, and before he had fairly attained his majority was a citizen of Illinois. His great fame as an orator and a statesman was attained as a citizen of that State, and his greatest triumphs, as well as his most crushing defeats, were achieved and received in his political contests with Lincoln in Illinois. As long as our Republic shall endure, so long will the memorable debates between these two distinguished sons of Illinois remain fresh in the memory of all students of American political history. From 1850 to the breaking out of the civil war no name was more conspicuous in the United States than that of Douglas. His contests in the Senate of the United States with such men as Chase and Hale, Seward and Sumner, Toombs and Breckinridge, had made him the most accomplished debater of his time and the recognized leader of the Democrats of the North.

Ulysses S. Grant, from the comparatively humble position of colonel of the Twenty-first Regiment of Illinois Volunteer Infantry, by his military genius and devotion to duty, rose from one military position to another until he became the general of all of the armies of the Federal forces during the late civil war and crowned his military achievements in the surrender of General Lee at Appomattox. His name as a military hero will forever rank with those of Alexander, Cæsar, and Napoleon. All of the other men whom I have mentioned were especially distinguished in their several ways, and all are well worthy of the recognition and honor which has been bestowed upon Miss WILLARD.

The question naturally arises then, How does this woman come to be selected for this especial recognition and honor? The story long antedates her birth and goes back to a period when Illinois was knocking at the doors of Congress for admission into the Union of States.

A distinguished historian has said that Daniel Webster was saved to his country more than one hundred years before his birth in the person of one of his direct ancestors—a little child, who at 4 years of age was saved from Indian massacre by having a washtub turned bottom side up over her, thus hiding her from a band of Indians who murdered all the other members of her family. So conditions for the development of the ability and character of Miss WILLARD were provided for in the legislation that relates to the admission of Illinois as a State into the Union long before her birth.

The northern limits of the Territory of Illinois were south of the south bend of Lake Michigan. Her population was principally from the States of Kentucky and Tennessee, North Carolina and Virginia. Her highways of commerce were the Illinois River, the Ohio, and the Mississippi. Her great commercial emporium was New Orleans, and the people of the slave-holding States her neighbors and friends. When she asked for admission into the Union, Judge Pope, her Congressional Delegate, proposed an amendment by which the northern limits of the proposed new State were extended northward 51 miles to the center of Lake Michigan, thence westward to the Mississippi River. The amendment included what are now the fourteen rich and populous northern counties of Illinois, including the great county of Cook, in which is located the imperial city of Chicago. Judge Pope, in advocating his amendment, pointed out that Illinois, if admitted as a State in the Union with the geographical limitations of the Territory, would have no business and commercial communication with the East and New England, and that her interests and her sympathies would naturally be with the South, and that in case of a contest between freedom and slavery, which he even then saw was inevitable, the fortunes of Illinois would naturally, by reason of friendship and interest, be with the Southern Confederacy.

The adoption of his amendment and the additional territory included would give the new State jurisdiction over the southwestern shores of Lake Michigan, and thereby unite it through the great waterway of the Lakes to Indiana, Ohio, Pennsylvania, New York, and New England; and that, ad-

mitted into the Union with this additional territory, she
might become the very keystone to perpetuate the Union.
Had Illinois been admitted as a State into the Union under
her territorial limitations we would never have had the Illinois and Michigan Canal, and the Illinois Central Railroad,
as it was constructed and has been operated, would never
have become an accomplished fact. Without these Chicago
would never have been the marvelous city that she is to-day,
and without the fourteen northern counties, settled as they
have been by people largely from New York and New England, Ohio, and Pennsylvania, the State of Illinois in 1854
would have been Democratic and would have supported
Stephen A. Douglas in his Kansas-Nebraska bill, and Governor Matteson, instead of Lyman Trumbull, would have
been elected to the United States Senate.

It was the vote of these fourteen counties that made the
State Republican in 1856 and made the candidacy of Abraham
Lincoln for the Presidency of the United States possible in
1860. It was the commingling within the limits of Illinois
of the civilizations represented by the settlers from Kentucky,
Tennessee, North Carolina, and Virginia with those of New
York, Pennsylvania, and New England that formed and de-
veloped the civic conditions in Illinois that proved so helpful
and healthful to the modest and timid nature of Miss WILLARD
when, as a mere schoolgirl, she left her country home in Wisconsin and came to Evanston, Ill., to acquire her education and
commence her life work.

This beautiful suburb of Chicago was her home for nearly
forty years. The conditions were all favorable here for the
unfolding not only of her superb intellect but of the splendid
qualities of character so marked in her mature life. Had she
lived and been educated in some sections of our country she

might have remained an instructor in some educational institution, where she would have been appreciated and honored as such, and have died loved and respected by the many students who were fortunate enough to come under her personal supervision, but unknown to the world.

In Evanston and Illinois the conditions were ripe for the exercise of the higher and better qualities of her nature, and when the demand came for her to lay aside what had been determined at one time to be her life work at the head of the Woman's College at the Northwestern University, she did not hesitate, although it seemed to many of her friends that she was making needless sacrifices in giving up an assured career as an instructor in that institution. God had intended her from the first for a greater work than that and for a wider field for the exercise of her great nature.

When she put aside the work of the schoolroom and entered the arena of the lecture platform in the cause of temperance and the purity of women, she entered the limelight of publicity, in which she remained during all the years of her great work in this and other countries. She did not escape the envious tongues of detractors nor the sharp thrusts of keen critics. She undertook tasks which to the average person would seem insurmountable, but to her only incidents in the career which she had marked out before her. Her labors, her successes, and her achievements have been eloquently portrayed here to-day by those who have preceded me. It is enough for me to note that no man or woman of her time wrought better or accomplished more for the protection and upbuilding of her sex and the cause of temperance. The endearments of home and the quiet of her fireside were sacrificed in the interest of the unfortunate among both men and women.

Her great soul carried her activities beyond State and national lines and led her to help the unfortunate in all countries
and all climes. The noble Roman matron Cornelia, when
called upon by a wealthy lady of Campania to exhibit to her
her jewels, called her two young sons to her side and said,
"These are my jewels." Miss WILLARD, who rejected the
offers of husband and home that she might the better serve
the cause to which she had dedicated her life, on a like request
for the exhibition of her jewels could have pointed to the
thousands of unfortunate men and women who had been res-
cued by her from lives of crime, drunkenness, and immorality
to that of pure womanhood and honorable manhood.

Her gentleness of heart, her charity, her firmness of principle,
and her attractive personality made her a power that attracted
to her the good women and men of this and other countries
that she visited and enabled her to accomplish a work that has
placed her name high on the list of the famous women of the
world. The work that she inaugurated is going on, and will
continue in augmented strength and influence so long as time
lasts.

It is not strange, then, Mr. President, that the people of Illinois should desire to see such a life and such a character especially honored. Her services have been world-wide. The
cause for which she dedicated her life reaches all humanity.
The ability with which she prosecuted this life work places her
among the most eminent intellects of our generation. She possessed all the qualities of organization which have made such
men as Marshall Field, Morgan, and Carnegie multimillionaires;
a genius which in military affairs would have made a general
of the first rank; legislative qualities which in the statesman
would have made his name historical; oratorical abilities which

have made such men as Beecher and Spurgeon immortal, and a charity which was heaven-born.

Illinois in thus honoring her to-day by placing her statue in yonder hall has honored herself and the women of our State and country. [Applause in the galleries.]

Address of Mr. Dolliver, of Iowa

Mr. PRESIDENT: There has been witnessed in the Capitol
to-day a scene the like of which has never taken place before—
thousands of children covering a statue with flowers and thousands of women standing before it in silence and in tears.

The original Hall of the House of Representatives has seen
strange vicissitudes. For two generations it was the arena in
which the great controversies of American politics were fought
out. Here the popular leaders of those times met in debate,
and within its walls the policies were shaped which entered into
the national life from the days of Jefferson to the period of
the civil war.

When the legislative chambers now occupied by the Senate
and House of Representatives were added to the Capitol their
earlier quarters were left to find other occupants and other
uses. The old Senate Chamber was given to the Supreme
Court, and while its appointments are somewhat meager for
that great tribunal, there is about it a certain atmosphere which
preserves all the great traditions of the place and makes it
seem appropriate for our court of last resort. The disposition
of the old Hall of the House of Representatives was not so
easy, for it lay right in the pathway of the multitude which
moves in restless procession through the main highway of
the Capitol. What to do with it puzzled alike the statesmen
and the architects.

At last they found a solution of the problem so desirable that
it was adopted without dissent. Congress dismissed the archi-

tects and resolved to preserve that historic apartment exactly as it was left to us by our fathers, nothing wanting except the mace and gavel to bring back the picture of the Chamber precisely as it looked to other generations, so that you can not walk through it to-day without hearing in your imagination the wondrous voice of Henry Clay, without listening to the fierce invectives of John Randolph of Roanoke, without seeing the young and eager face of David Wilmot, without feeling the hush of silence amid the confusion of the day, as you pause to look at the brass tablet on the floor which records the glorious exit of John Quincy Adams from the noise and strife of time.

It is not strange that everybody acquiesced, seeing that it could not be taken from the people, in the proposal to set the place apart, to be kept forever as a memorial hall, no longer for the living, but for the august assembly of the dead. One by one its vacant spaces have been chosen by the States entitled to them, until now these solemn effigies stand close together like a family reunion of the great ones of the earth. More than twenty of the States are represented, though some, even among the oldest, have not felt like choosing among their honored citizens the names which are to stand in such distinct preeminence. Statesmen and orators are there, secure in their renown. Soldiers are there, with sword in hand. Inventors are there, whose ingenuity gave practical ideas to the world; and priests to bless them all with the benediction of their holy office.

We are met to-day to put in place another pedestal; to accept another statue donated by the people to the nation. It is brought here by a State rich in the household treasures of its biography—the State which gave to American politics the leadership of Stephen A. Douglas; the State from which Abra-

ham Lincoln set out on his triumphal journey to the capital;
the State which signed the first commission of General Grant;
the State in which John A. Logan was born, and from which
he went forth to become the ideal volunteer soldier of the
Republic. Yet the great Commonwealth passes all these by
and brings here, with reverence and pride, a work of art so full
of gentleness and grace that all the illustrious company about
it seem to bow with stately ceremony before the white figure
of this elect daughter of Illinois—FRANCES E. WILLARD.
[Applause in the galleries.]

I have seen in the newspapers more than one sneering comment upon the action of the general assembly in choosing a
woman to represent the State in our National Statuary Hall,
and I have heard the sneer repeated here at the Capitol in
thoughtless conversation. I confess that to me a criticism such
as that seems strangely out of place; and in the light of what
has been witnessed here to-day it seems too paltry and absurd
even for passing notice.

The distinguished Senator from Illinois [Mr. Cullom] has
spoken so fully of the life and high achievements of Miss
WILLARD that it would be inappropriate for me to repeat the
story of her career. He knew her well. I was acquainted
with her only in a distant way, and was less familiar than perhaps I ought to have been with the work which she was doing
in the world. So that it would be impossible for me, even if
it were appropriate, to speak of her as he has spoken.

I knew her only as a public teacher and most distinctly as
a factor in the political controversies of our times. It was
my fortune to hear her more than once, advocating before
the people her favorite reforms.

She was one of the most persuasive orators who ever spoke
our tongue, and her influence, apart from the singular beauty

of her character, rested upon that fine art of reaching the hearts and consciences of men which gave her a right to the leadership which she exercised for so many years. I remember once hearing her speak, when General Harrison was a candidate for the Presidency, in Norumbega Hall, at Bangor, Me. I was on the stump for the Republican candidate and shared in a full measure the impatience of my own party with those who, under their sense of duty, were engaged in turning our voters aside in an effort to build up an organization of their own, pledged to the prohibition of the liquor traffic in America.

I remember that I was especially irritated because the party which Miss WILLARD represented was not willing to let us alone in Maine.

Notwithstanding all my prejudices, I invited a friend, a hardened politician, then famous in our public life, to go with me to hear Miss WILLARD speak. He reluctantly consented upon condition that we should take a back seat and go out when he indicated that he had had enough. For more than two hours this gifted woman, with marvelous command of language, with a delicate sense of the fitness and simplicity of words, with a perfect understanding of the secret places of the human heart, moved that great multitude with a skill that belongs to genius alone, and to genius only when it is touched with live coals from the altar. And when it was all over we agreed together that in all our lives we had never witnessed a display so marvelous of intellectual and spiritual power.

But it is not my purpose to pronounce a eulogy upon Miss WILLARD. A life like hers, given without reservation and without terms to help and to bless the world, is in no need of empty words of praise. It is crowned already beyond all our poor eulogies.

I do not know whether her devoted followers in Illinois, who presented to the legislature the petition asking that she be selected for this immortal honor, had in their thought everything which this statue means. They were moved, I do not doubt, by the love which they had for her to claim for her memory this national recognition. But even if love for her and generous appreciation of her distinguished civic services were the only motives which actuated the people of Illinois, there remains a larger significance which belongs to this occasion, of which I desire to speak.

The appearance of this statue in the Capitol of the United States is not only a tribute to the career "of an illustrious person," to use the language of the statute; it is also a visible token of a forward movement in modern society which has already made a new statement of the relation of the home to the State, in terms so unmistakable that the womanhood of America, long since familiar with the burdens of a larger responsibility, has entered at last into a larger opportunity.

I am not going to discuss and I do not even feel bound to give my opinion upon some of the questions to which FRANCES E. WILLARD devoted the latter years of her life. She was, most of us think, a pioneer, and whether the lands which she explored are to be occupied to-morrow, or the next day, or the next century, I will not even stop to inquire.

These things are less important than some have thought, and will be worked out in woman's way and woman's time. But there are noticeable signs of the times, which Miss WILLARD at once illustrated and interpreted, that may be spoken of without venturing into the field of controversy.

A college graduate, a student pursuing her studies in the University of Paris, worthily wearing her academic robes, she was a forerunner of the unnumbered host of American young women who have captured the prizes of every college and university that has dared to admit them, until they have threatened at last to leave to their brethren no certificates of superiority except the doubtful credentials of the athletic field.

Already they have taken possession of the high schools of America, and those of us who have had a chance, as I have often had, to look in on graduating exercises in city or in village, finding in every class a dozen strong and healthy girls and an average of about three boys, one of them lame and the others very pale, have been compelled to entertain disquieting thoughts about the future of man's monopoly in those worldly affairs which require a preliminary training of the mind.

Under such circumstances it would be strange if American women had not already knocked at the doors of all professions and of all the other honorable pursuits of life. She has not hesitated to attempt the practice of the law. She has successfully acquired the learning of all the schools of medicine. She has challenged the church to show cause why she ought not to be commissioned to unfold to others the mysteries of the godliness of which she is the most perfect disciple. She has become the patroness of art, of literature, and of those far-reaching philanthropies which are lifting the world out of paganism and barbarism, and casting up a highway for the progress of civilization.

Into this new world this daughter of Illinois was born. With a woman's intuition she grasped the meaning of her surroundings. Turning aside from the ostentations of society, she put away from her the endearments of domestic life, the sweet content of home and children, and offered her whole strength to the Master whom she served that she might help the needy, feed the hungry, lift up the fallen, and throw the

protection of our institutions about the firesides of the
American people. I think her largest influence will be associated with the work of the Woman's Christian Temperance
Union, and I can not speak of that without a sincere feeling
when I remember one near and dear whose life was wrapped up
in the benign purposes and plans of that great organization.

Lord Macaulay said of John Wesley that he was one of
the greatest statesmen of his time. What did he mean by
that? He meant that in addition to his preaching the Word
he created an institution, compact and effective in its methods, which went on long after he was gone, in the execution
of the beneficent designs which were in his heart. Exactly
the same thing can be said for FRANCES E. WILLARD. And
she owed to that organization possibly more even than she
knew, because the position which she held in it made her
office a central bureau to which reports were made of the
moral and intellectual signs of the times; and no man can
read her annual messages to the organization of which she
was the executive head without perceiving that she had a
strong grasp of all the great social and moral problems of
our time; a grasp so strong that to-day her words seem
often like prophecies fulfilled, where twenty years ago they
hardly attracted the attention of the world.

I think the highest point in the public career of the late
Senator Hanna was that last speech of his before a meeting
of laboring men and capitalists belonging to the Civic Fed-
eration in New York. When standing there, without any
pretensions to piety or sanctity of any sort, he laid down
the proposition, based on a long experience as a laborer and
an employer, and on an intimate acquaintance with the leaders of political thought in all parties, that the rights of labor
and the rights of capital can never be established on a last-

ing basis of justice except as both bow in loyal obedience to the law of Christ. FRANCES E. WILLARD had, for twenty years before her death, taught that doctrine, not only in its application to the labor question, but to all the complex social problems of these times.

Her chief title as a teacher of social and moral science lies in this: With a profound insight she perceived that the most difficult problems of civilization, the problems which have brought the statesmanship and philosophy of the modern world to a dead standstill, if they have any solution at all — and she confidently believed they had — they would find it at last in the actual application to the daily life of the world of the divine precepts which constitute the most precious part of the inheritance of these Christian centuries. [Applause in the galleries.]

And so I think that the general assembly of Illinois did well to set up this monument in memory of her. The children who have covered it this day with flowers have paid to her a tribute so simple and so appropriate that its fragrance will fill these corridors long after the formal ceremonies of this hour have been forgotten. And in after generations, as long as this venerable edifice remains, the women of America, as they look upon the chiseled beauty of that face, standing like a goddess among our heroes and our sages, will whisper a word of gratitude to the people of Illinois when they remember the act of her general assembly, which, careless alike of custom and of precedent, has added to the title of their citizenship this perpetual dignity in the Capitol of the United States. [Applause in the galleries.]

The PRESIDENT pro tempore. The question is on agreeing to the resolutions submitted by the Senator from Illinois [Mr. Cullom], which will be read.

The Secretary again read the resolutions.

The resolutions were unanimously agreed to.

Mr. CULLOM.   I move that the Senate adjourn.

The motion was agreed to; and (at 4 o'clock and 32 minutes p. m.) the Senate adjourned its legislative session until to-morrow, Saturday, February 18, 1905, at 12 o'clock meridian.

FEBRUARY 20, 1905.

The PRESIDENT pro tempore. The Chair lays before the Senate a concurrent resolution from the House of Representatives, which will be read, and to which he calls the attention of the Senator from Illinois [Mr. Cullom].

The Secretary read the resolution, as follows:

Resolved by the House of Representatives (the Senate concurring), That the statue of FRANCES E. WILLARD, presented by the State of Illinois, to be placed in Statuary Hall, be accepted by the United States, and that the thanks of Congress be tendered the State for the statue of one of the most eminent women of the United States.

Resolved, That a copy of these resolutions, duly authenticated, be transmitted to the governor of the State of Illinois.

Mr. CULLOM. Mr. President, a similar resolution has already passed the Senate, but the other House has passed the concurrent resolution which has just been read. I ask unanimous consent for the consideration of the House concurrent resolution at this time.

The resolution was considered by unanimous consent, and agreed to.

Proceedings in the House

⌒

JANUARY 19, 1905.

STATUE OF FRANCES E. WILLARD.

The Speaker laid before the House the following communication:

The Clerk read as follows:

STATE OF ILLINOIS, EXECUTIVE DEPARTMENT,
Springfield, January 10, 1905.

DEAR SIR: Governor Deneen is in receipt of a letter from the chairman of the Illinois board of commissioners for the FRANCES E. WILLARD statue, informing him that the sculptor, Helen Farnsworth Mears, reports that the model will reach Washington, D. C., on February 11. The commissioners express the desire that Governor Deneen advise the Senate of the United States and House of Representatives of the completion of the statue in order that a date may be immediately fixed for its acceptance by Congress. I am directed by Governor Deneen to communicate this fact to you for your information and such action as Congress may see fit to take.

Yours, truly,

J. WHITTAKER,
Secretary.

Hon. JOS. G. CANNON,
Speaker House of Representatives,
Washington, D. C.

Mr. Foss. Mr. Speaker, I ask unanimous consent for the present consideration of the following resolution.

The SPEAKER. The gentleman from Illinois [Mr. Foss] asks unanimous consent for the present consideration of a resolution, which the Clerk will report.

The Clerk read as follows:

Resolved, That the exercises appropriate to the reception and acceptance from the State of Illinois of the statue of FRANCES E. WILLARD, erected in Statuary Hall in the Capitol, be made the special order for Friday, February 17, at 4 o'clock.

Mr. McCLEARY, of Minnesota. Mr. Speaker, I would like to ask whether this statue is one of the two that each State is authorized to erect in Statuary Hall?

Mr. Foss. It is.

The SPEAKER. Is there objection?

There was no objection.

The resolution was agreed to.

Memorial Exercises

Friday, February 17, 1905.

The House met at 12 o'clock noon.

The Chaplain, Rev. Henry N. Couden, D. D., offered the following prayer:

We lift up our hearts in gratitude to Thee, O God, our Heavenly Father, for this day, which marks an epoch in the progress and civilization of our age and nation by the placing of the statue of a woman in this Capitol, among the noted and illustrious men of our nation, who, by the purity of her soul, the breadth and scope of her intellectual attainments, the eloquence and chastity of her speech, and her unselfish devotion to the purity of the home, the State, the nation, and humanity, won for herself the splendid and just encomium, "The uncrowned queen of purity and temperance." God grant that there it may stand instinct with life and vocal with its eloquent appeal "for God and home and native land;" there may it stand a beacon light for untold millions in their upward and onward march toward the ideals in Christian manhood and womanhood; and glory and praise be Thine, through Jesus Christ our Lord. Amen.

RESERVATION OF GALLERY.

Mr. Foss. Mr. Speaker, I ask unanimous consent that the following resolution be agreed to.

The SPEAKER. The Clerk will read the resolution.

The Clerk read as follows:

Resolved, That during the ceremonies incident to the acceptance of the statue of FRANCES E. WILLARD presented by the State of Illinois to the Government of the United States, on Friday, February 17, at 4 o'clock, the southeast ladies' gallery be reserved for the Illinois statuary commission and the relatives of the late FRANCES E. WILLARD and such citizens of Illinois as may attend these services.

The SPEAKER. Is there objection?

There was no objection.

ACCEPTANCE OF STATUE OF FRANCES E. WILLARD.

The SPEAKER. The Clerk will read the special order.

The Clerk read as follows:

Friday, February 17.—On motion of Mr. Foss, by unanimous consent, *Resolved*, That the exercises appropriate to the reception and acceptance from the State of Illinois of the statue of FRANCES E. WILLARD, erected in Statuary Hall, in the Capitol, be made the special order for Friday, February 17, at 4 o'clock.

Mr. Foss. Mr. Speaker, I will ask the Clerk to read the communication which I send to the desk.

The Clerk read as follows:

EXECUTIVE DEPARTMENT,
Springfield, February 16, 1905.

To the Senate and House of Representatives of the United States:

By authority of the act of the general assembly of Illinois the governor of Illinois heretofore appointed Anna E. Gordon, Mary E. Metzgar, John J. Mitchell, W. R. Jewell, and Mrs. S. M. D. Fry to constitute a commission to procure a statue of FRANCES E. WILLARD for erection in Statuary Hall, in the Capitol at Washington, D. C.

I am informed by the commissioners that the statue was made by Helen F. Mears, of New York City; that it is completed and has been placed in position and is now ready to be presented to Congress.

I have been further informed by Miss Anna E. Gordon, chairman of the commissioners, that a resolution is to be presented accepting said statue. As governor of the State of Illinois, therefore, I have the honor to present to the Government of the United States the statue hereinbefore referred to.

Very respectfully,

CHAS. S. DENEEN,
Governor of Illinois.

Mr. Foss. Mr. Speaker, I submit the following resolution, which I send to the desk, and ask that it be considered as pending.

The Clerk read as follows:

Resolved by the House of Representatives (the Senate concurring), That the statue of FRANCES E. WILLARD, presented by the State of Illinois, to be placed in Statuary Hall, be accepted by the United States, and that the thanks of Congress be tendered the State for the statue of one of the most eminent women of the United States.

Resolved, That a copy of these resolutions, duly authenticated, be transmitted to the governor of the State of Illinois.

Address of Mr. Foss, of Illinois

◈

Mr. SPEAKER: Congress, on July 2, 1864, passed a law authorizing the President to invite all the States to provide and furnish statues in marble or bronze, not exceeding two in number for each State, of deceased persons who have been citizens thereof and illustrious for their historic renown or for distinguished civic or military service, such as each State may deem to be worthy of this national commemoration, and when so furnished the same shall be placed in the old Hall of the House of Representatives in the Capitol of the United States, which is set apart, or so much thereof as may be necessary, as a National Statuary Hall.

In pursuance of this, nineteen States have presented statues of illustrious citizens; fourteen States have filled their quota:

Massachusetts, Winthrop and Adams.

New Hampshire, Stark and Webster.

Vermont, Collamer and Allen.

Rhode Island, Greene and Williams.

Connecticut, Sherman and Trumbull.

New York, Clinton and Livingston.

New Jersey, Stockton and Kearny.

Pennsylvania, Fulton and Muhlenberg.

Maryland, Carroll and Hanson.

West Virginia, Kenna and Pierpont.

Ohio, Allen and Garfield.

Missouri, Benton and Blair.

Texas, Houston and Austin.

Maine, King.

Indiana, Morton.

Michigan, Cass.

Wisconsin, Marquette.

Kansas, Ingalls.

Illinois has her Shields, and now presents the statue of
FRANCES E. WILLARD, one of the foremost women of her time.

The following act was passed by the legislature of Illinois
with practical unanimity on February 28, 1899, and signed by
the governor:

Whereas Congress has invited each State of the Union to furnish statues
in marble or bronze of two of its deceased citizens, illustrious for their
historic renown or for distinguished civic or military service, and deemed
worthy of national commemoration, and to have the same placed in the
National Statuary Hall, in the Capitol, at Washington, D. C.; and

Whereas the State of Illinois has furnished but one of its statues, and
before the close of this century it should complete the number allotted to
it; and

Whereas Illinois has been noted for its illustrious warriors, jurists, and
statesmen—Grant, Shields, Logan, Palmer, McClernand, Davis, Trumbull,
Breese, Schofield, McAllister, Lincoln, Douglas, Yates, Lovejoy, and countless others, like McDougall and Baker, who won fame in other States; and

Whereas the fame of none of these was more heroically won or more
richly deserved than that of one of our deceased citizens, illustrious for
historic renown and distinguished for civic service in Europe and America
in a new unexplored field of Christian endeavor, the effect of whose efforts
and achievements and the influence of whose spotless life and sublime
example has been so marked that the world has wondered and admired
the author, organizer, and advocate of purity and temperance, Illinois's
most illustrious deceased citizen, FRANCES E. WILLARD, the uncrowned
queen of purity and temperance, whose ashes repose in peace on the shores
of Lake Michigan at Evanston, Ill. Her life, like that of her Redeemer,
was devoted to the spiritual welfare of mankind, and the world at large
has been materially benefited by her prayers and sacrifices. Radiant
with a halo of all the virtues, her face shown with the light of intelligence.
Her marvelous abilities energized all around and about her, while her
gentleness, tact, and self-sacrificing spirit calmed every storm that rose in
the councils which were graced and blessed by her presence. Her grand
life is a "beacon light" to the good and the true of all sexes, races, and
creeds in the civilized world, and her wonderful achievements are lights

and landmarks on the cliffs of fame, which will for all time illumine the paths of millions of women wherever civilization has a footing, which is where woman is duly appreciated; and

Whereas the priceless heritage of such a life belongs of right to Illinois; and

Whereas she glories in it, and deems it "worthy of national commemoration:" Therefore,

To immortalize it, and to show all nations how exalted a sphere woman occupies in this great State, the following law is hereby placed upon our statute books:

AN ACT to select commissioners to expend not to exceed $9,000 in purchasing a heroic bronze or marble statue of the late FRANCES E. WILLARD, and to provide a pedestal to be appropriately inscribed and ornamented, and also to defray the expense of transporting the same to Washington, D. C., when completed, and erecting it in the National Statuary Hall at Washington, D. C.

Be it enacted by the people of the State of Illinois represented in the general assembly, That five persons, to be selected by the governor of the State, be, and they are hereby, authorized and empowered, as commissioners, to purchase a heroic statue of the late FRANCES E. WILLARD, to be cast in standard bronze metal or marble, and a pedestal or base for the same, and also to defray the cost and expenses of transporting them when completed to Washington, D. C., and erecting them in the National Statuary Hall at the Capitol, said commissioners shall not hereby be empowered to obligate the State of Illinois to pay any amount in excess of the sum stated in section 3 of this act.

SEC. 2. Said commissioners are to receive no pay nor compensation of any kind for their services in the fulfillment of duties required of them by this act.

SEC. 3. For the purpose of defraying the cost of said statue, pedestal, and all other costs and obligations hereinbefore stated and set forth, or incident thereto, the sum of $9,000, or so much thereof as may be necessary, is hereby appropriated out of the State treasury, and the auditor of public accounts is hereby required to draw his warrant on the treasurer of the State for such sum as may be expended, upon bills of particulars, to be approved of by the governor.

The commissioners appointed by the governor were Miss Anna A. Gordon, Evanston; John J. Mitchell, Chicago; Mrs. Susanna M. D. Fry, Evanston; W. R. Jewell, Danville; and Mrs. Mary E. Metzgar, Moline.

The commissioners awarded the execution of the statue to Helen Farnsworth Mears, and she has brought out in Carrara marble the refined womanliness, the nobility and strength of character, the sweetness and simplicity, and the intense yearning to help humanity which characterized FRANCES E. WILLARD as an educator, philanthropist, and friend.

The statue is of Carrara marble, a little more than life size, and represents Miss WILLARD standing in an easy, graceful position. The right arm is slightly extended, the hand resting upon a reading desk; the left arm is at her side with a few pages of manuscript in the hand. The pose of the head is very lifelike as Miss WILLARD appeared when looking out upon an audience. The face is strong and spiritual.

The pedestal is of Vermont marble and bears the following inscription:

"Ah! it is women who have given the costliest hostages to fortune. Out into the battle of life they have sent their best beloved, with fearful odds against them. Oh, by the dangers they have dared; by the hours of patient watching over beds where helpless children lay; by the incense of ten thousand prayers wafted from their gentle lips to heaven, I charge you give them power to protect along life's treacherous highway those whom they have so loved."—FRANCES E. WILLARD.

PRESENTED BY THE STATE OF ILLINOIS,

FEBRUARY XVII, MCMV.

In pursuance of a resolution adopted by the House of Representatives on January 19, 1905, which I, as Representative of the district in which FRANCES E. WILLARD lived, had the honor to introduce, we are here assembled at this hour to receive and accept from the State of Illinois the statue of this noble woman, now erected in Statuary Hall.

FRANCES E. WILLARD was of New England ancestry. She was born in 1839, in the little village of Churchville, about 14 miles west of the city of Rochester, N. Y. When but 3 years of age her parents moved to Oberlin, Ohio, and five years afterwards they settled in Wisconsin, near the town of Janesville, where her father purchased a large farm on the banks of Rock River, and here she spent twelve years of her life. At the age of 17 she entered the female college of Milwaukee, where her aunt was professor of history, and remained there a year, and then pursued her studies further at the Woman's College of the Northwestern University, at Evanston. She stood at the head of her class and became editor of the college paper, and was a natural leader among her companions. Upon graduation she chose the profession of a teacher, and had she continued would have made one of the great teachers of the country, as she had a natural fitness for this work. For a time she taught at a female college in Pittsburg, Pa., and at the Genesee Wesleyan Seminary, Lima, N. Y.

After a two years' trip abroad she returned to Evanston, her home, and was elected dean of the Woman's College there, where she worked with great success for three years. Then she resigned her position and entered upon the greater work to which she was called.

She became president of a Chicago Woman's Christian Temperance Society, and soon after prepared her first lecture on "The New Chivalry," which produced such favorable comment that she was besieged with a large number of engagements to speak, and thus began her career as a public speaker.

Miss Anna A. Gordon, in her work on The Beautiful Life of Frances E. Willard, states that—

> The story of Miss WILLARD's early Chicago work reads like a romance. Into it she flung herself with the ardor of a St. Francis d'Assisi. She made the little great, the weak a power. She who had studied books now studied humanity.

In October of the same year she was the moving spirit in the organization of the Illinois Woman's Christian Temperance Union, and in November following she assisted in the organization of the National Woman's Christian Temperance Union at Cleveland, Ohio, and became its secretary, so that within a few brief months after the choice of her career we find her an active force in the local, State, and national unions. In 1879 she was elected president of the national union, and was reelected year after year until she died.

In 1883, with Anna A. Gordon, her devoted friend and assistant, she visited every State and Territory in the Union, traveling 30,000 miles and organizing local unions everywhere. In the same year Miss WILLARD founded the World's Christian Temperance Union and became its president. She visited England in 1892 and was given a great reception in London, participated in by fifty philanthropical societies and some of the foremost men of Great Britain. She returned home and pursued her work with greater zeal and energy until she departed this life in the city of New York February 17, 1898 — seven years ago to-day.

Time would fail me to describe the wonderful work accomplished by this woman. Edward Everett Hale, in his tribute to her, said:

Miss WILLARD has commanded and deserved the love and respect of millions of the women of this country. With unanimous loyalty, enthusiastic wherever they could express it, they chose her every year to be the president of their great temperance organization, whose work under her leadership has been extraordinary. Its history thus far has been the same thing as the biography of FRANCES WILLARD. That history is not simply the narrative of a noble life. It is an important illustration of wise administration. Her annual messages to her constituents are better worth reading than the messages of the President of the United States for the same time. They were messages to people she loved and who loved her, written with the enthusiasm of love letters by a woman singularly well educated, broad in her whole view of life, and in her very heart, and in every syllable which her heart prompted, brave and true.

The Woman's Christian Temperance Union, of which Miss WILLARD was the controlling spirit, is the greatest organization of Christian women ever banded together for a great cause.

It grew out of the great woman's temperance crusade of 1873–74. It has sixty-four auxiliary unions; fifty-six are State, and six are Territorial, and the other two are the District of Columbia and Hawaii. It has been organized in every State and Territory of the nation, and locally in 10,000 towns and cities. Its national motto is: "For God, for home, and native land." Its badge is the white ribbon, symbolical of purity and peace and the preservation of the home. Its principles are: "To educate the young; to form a better public sentiment; to reform, so far as possible, by religious, ethical, and scientific means, the drinking classes; to seek the transforming power of divine grace for ourselves and all for whom we work, that they and we may willfully transcend no law of pure and wholesome living; and finally we pledge ourselves to labor and to pray that all these principles, founded upon the Gospel and Christ, may be worked out into the customs of society and the laws of the land."

The World's Woman's Christian Temperance Union is composed of national unions which have been organized in over fifty nations, with a total membership of about half a million. These facts give a better idea than anything else of the great work which has been accomplished by FRANCES WILLARD, the founder of the Woman's Christian Temperance Union.

Above all things FRANCES WILLARD was an organizer. She organized for women through women. She often said:

Alone we can do little, separated we are the units of weakness, but aggregated we become batteries of power. Agitate, educate, organize— these are the deathless watchwords of success.

Whittier has summed up her life work in these lines:

> She knew the power of banded ill,
> But felt that love was stronger still,
> And organized, for doing good,
> The world's united womanhood.

[Applause.]

FRANCES WILLARD was an orator. She had the gift of eloquence to a remarkable degree. Both Beecher and Phillips have paid tribute to her power over audiences. Her voice was clear and penetrating and had in it that peculiar quality which held her audience entranced. She had a message and she told it with great simplicity, but with greater power. Gunsaulus and Hillis, two of the most eloquent preachers of our day, have testified to her powers of oratory. The former said:

If a great heart, fed by fiery streams from on high, glowing and molten with burning love for humanity, issuing forth its indignant denunciation of evil, pouring out incessant streams of argument against well-dressed error and fashionable wrong, kindling with lightning-like heat thousands of fellow-beings until they also flash to holy wrath which scathes the slayer and illumines the slain; if lifting millions of human beings from out the noise and dullness of unreason into the serene radiance of reason, so that they are willing to obey the highest ideals and to serve at any cost the noblest demands of humanity and God; if these be the characteristics or results of eloquence, then, without doubt, FRANCES WILLARD must be considered one of the most eloquent of the orators of our time.

Hillis has said:

Her greatest oratorical triumphs were in villages and cities, where some hall not holding more than a thousand people was crowded with appreciative listeners. At such times she stood forth one of the most gifted speakers of this generation, achieving efforts that were truly amazing. What ease and grace of bearing! What gentleness and strength! What pathos and sympathy! How exquisitely modulated her words! If her speech did not flow as a gulf stream; if it did not beat like an ocean upon a continent, she sent her sentences forth, an arrowy flight, and each tipped with divine fire.

FRANCES WILLARD was universally mourned as one of the greatest women of her time. Bishop Newman said of her:

For intelligence and eloquence she was the foremost woman of her generation. Such was the breadth of her catholicity that she recognized goodness wherever found. Her philanthropy touched suffering humanity in all lands. * * * Let womanhood emulate her virtues, imitate her example, cherish her memory, till purity and temperance shall become coextensive with the business and abode of humanity.

Bishop Fallows said:

I have heard many women—women who have achieved greatness—but never have I heard one who was so finished and eloquent as the dead leader of the great temperance movement among women. * * * There was but one Miss WILLARD. * * * She is worthy to rank with Jefferson, for she formulated a declaration of independence for her sex.

Bishop Vincent said:

FRANCES WILLARD was a dreamer and a doer. She saw visions and wrought them into orations and devices and achievements.

Doctor Barrows said:

Her grand life is a prophecy and harbinger of the good time which has been so long on the way. Miss WILLARD will be mourned in all the continents. I found her name as familiar and dear in Asia as in America.

John D. Long, speaking of her life, said:

It has been a life of devotion to humanity. Her services in the cause of temperance and good morals have been of inestimable value. Her example and influence will henceforth be a part of the forces molding the advancing civilization of our country and the world.

Dr. Josiah Strong said:

She was one of the great women of the world, and made all people her debtors.

Anthony Comstock said:

Earth has been enriched by her life and presence.

Canon Wilberforce paid tribute also to her personal influence, her platform gifts, her wonderful power of organization, and her single-heartedness.

Rev. F. W. Farrar, dean of Canterbury, said:

Miss WILLARD set a very noble example of self-denying labor on behalf of a great cause, and she showed how grand a work may be achieved by a single-hearted toiler inspired by the love of God and man.

Dr. George C. Lorimer has said:

If Miss WILLARD had been a man she would have rivaled Cobden and Bright in philanthropic statesmanship; if she had been a man she would have excelled Adam Smith in promoting the wealth of nations; if she had been a man she would have ranked with Wilberforce and Garrison in

advancing the cause of emancipation; if she had been a man she would
have shared the laurels of Carnot the elder as an organizer of armies and
of Grant as their persistent and successful commander. But being a
woman—well, posterity, I am sure, will assign her a unique niche in the
temple of fame.

The State of Illinois presents this statue as a tribute to the
life of FRANCES E. WILLARD, and in a larger and truer sense
as a tribute to woman and the magnificent progress she has
made under our free institutions.

The past century has been one of great progress in art, in
literature, in science, in all things; not that it has produced
the greatest poets in the world, nor the greatest authors, nor
the greatest orators, but the century will be conspicuous in
that education, enlightenment, and advancement have come
to the many and not to the few. But the greatest progress
has been that of woman.

Mrs. John Adams, a little over a hundred years ago, in
speaking of the women of her time, said that "female education in the best families went no further than writing and
arithmetic, and in some few and rare instances music and
dancing." What a marvelous change has been wrought in the
succeeding years in the education of woman.

Oberlin College, in Ohio, was the first institution to grant
a diploma to women, in 1838. Since then the highest institutions, with few exceptions, have been thrown open to
both sexes, and are granting degrees to women in theological,
medical, and legal schools, and the world has marked the
magnificent progress which woman has made.

A few years ago Susan B. Anthony in an article said that
"fifty years ago woman in the United States was without a
recognized individuality in any department of life," but now we
find her in all occupations and in all professions dividing honors
with men.

It might be asked, Why should the State of Illinois, which has produced so many illustrious men, offer the statue of a woman, the first to be placed in yonder hall among warriors and statesmen and pioneers and discoverers, who have wrought mightily for their country on the field of battle, in the halls of Congress, on the frontier, and in civil life? Why did not Illinois send here a statue of Lincoln, that divinely gifted man whom James Russell Lowell called "the first American," or why should she not place here in yonder hall the statue of the great Douglas, whose life was interwoven with that of Lincoln, the two mighty antagonists in the greatest debate of modern times?

Some might ask, Why not place there the statue of Ulysses S. Grant, the foremost general of the century, a man who wrought nobly for the salvation of his country and the preservation of the Union, and no sooner had the war clouds disappeared than he became the great advocate of peace, a perpetual peace between all sections of our common country in the eternal bonds of American brotherhood? [Applause.]

But these great men of Illinois whom I have named belonged to no State, but were given long since to the Union. No statue can ever add to their fame, and no monument can ever tower as high as the magnificent character which they left to their country. Why confine them within the bounds of Statuary Hall? They have stood for many a year out under the American sky, the dome of the everlasting Union, and received the veneration of every American citizen for the mighty works which they wrought in the nation's life.

The Illinois legislature, without the slightest disrespect to her great sons, in its wisdom believed that the time had come when woman should be honored and when her statue should be placed in the American Pantheon, and who shall say that woman has no right there? [Applause.] What voice will be lifted to protest? Has all the wonderful development of our country ever since the time when that frail bark landed with its precious cargo of human freight on Plymouth Rock been accomplished by men? Has woman played no part in this tremenduous national development? Has she exercised no influence on our national life?

Who does not recall the bravery of those noble women who endured the hardships and deprivations of life, for conscience' sake, along with their fathers, their husbands, and their brothers in the first few years of the Plymouth colony? And all along down through the history of our country has not woman been the companion of man in the trials and tribulations, in peace and in war, doing her part as nobly as he, laying the foundations of the state, and building upon them a government of liberty, equality, and fraternity to all?

Time would fail me to enumerate many instances where woman has played a conspicuous part in our national history. Who does not recall Molly Pitcher, who fired the last gun at Fort Clinton, and afterwards received a lieutenant's commission from Washington?

Who does not recall Catharine Schuyler setting fire to the grain fields for fear that the British might reap the harvest? Who does not recall Narcissa Whitman, the first white woman to settle in the State of Washington, who, with her husband, Dr. Marcus Whitman, went as a missionary to the Indians and lost her life in the opening up of the far western country? Who does not recall how the early mothers wrought in the development of the mighty West everywhere? How they endured the hardships and braved the dangers of life in the paths of civilization and builded the home and planted the sanctuary and worshiped their God out on the outposts of civilization, which later became the fortifications of freedom, of liberty, and enlightenment. [Applause.]

Nor, sir, can we forget the gentle ministering angels of the camps and hospitals during our wars, and particularly during our great civil war. On one side or on the other, for while there was a division of sentiment between two sections of our great country there was no sectionalism in the gentleness and the thoughtfulness of the ministrations of the American woman whether she lived in the North or in the South [applause], and many a northern soldier had his wounds bound up and went on his way through the attention and care of the noble women of the South. [Applause.]

American history indeed would not be complete without mentioning the name of Harriet Beecher Stowe, who, through the mutterings of Uncle Tom, awoke the conscience of the people to "man's injustice to man," and Julia Ward Howe, whose famous Battle Hymn of the Republic stirred the souls of men to victory, and Clara Barton [applause], who helped to bind the wounds which war had made.

In every field of human endeavor she has nobly done her part. Why, the mere mention of the names of Mary Lyon, Margaret Fuller, Harriet Martineau, Susan B. Anthony, Lucy Stone, Harriet Hosmer, Charlotte Cushman, Mary Livermore, Lucretia Mott, Elizabeth Stuart Phelps, Elizabeth Cady Stanton, Helen Keller, Helen Gould, Bertha Palmer, Jane Addams, and others I might mention call to mind the influence and power of woman in the development of American civilization. [Applause.]

Nor should I forget that woman above all other women, whose life and all its energies are consecrated to the home; who quietly and patiently wends her way without any other thought than the development of the young life or lives around her, who in after years may rise to call her blessed; content to live, perchance, in a narrow sphere, educating her children, fitting them for higher stations in life than she ever hoped to occupy, giving them advantages she never could have, inspired by that one great thought of doing for those she loved—I refer to that noble woman whom each man calls "mother." [Applause.]

How often do we hear men who have achieved the greatest success in human life with one accord turn and say that their success is due to her. Perhaps no instance is so conspicuous in recent years as that of our martyred McKinley. What poet can say proper tribute, what author can give full praise, or what orator can ever describe the height and depth of a mother's love? She, after all, has been the mighty controlling influence in our national life. [Applause.]

FRANCES E. WILLARD herself once said: "If I were asked what was the true mission of the ideal woman, I would say, 'It is to make the whole world motherlike.'"

Illinois, therefore, presents this statue, not only as a tribute to her whom it represents—one of the foremost women of America—but as a tribute to woman and her mighty influence upon our national life; to woman in the home; to woman in all the occupations and professions of life; to woman in all her charity and philanthropy, wherever she is toiling for the good of humanity; to woman everywhere, who has ever stood "for God, for home, for native land." [Great applause.]

Address of Mr. Graff, of Illinois

Mr. SPEAKER: The legislature of the State of Illinois passed an act which was approved by Governor John R. Tanner, February 28, 1899, entitled "An act to select a commission to expend not to exceed $9,000 to purchase a heroic bronze or marble statue of the late FRANCES E. WILLARD, and to provide a pedestal, to be appropriately inscribed and ornamented, and also to defray the expenses of transportation of same to Washington, D. C., when completed, and erecting it in the National Statuary Hall" in this city. The preamble of that act reads as follows:

Whereas Congress has invited each State of the Union to furnish statues in marble or bronze of two of its deceased citizens, illustrious for their historic renown or for distinguished civic or military service, and deemed worthy of national commemoration, and to have the same placed in the National Statuary Hall in the Capitol at Washington, D. C.; and

Whereas the State of Illinois has furnished but one of its statues, and before the close of the century should complete the number allotted to it; and

Whereas Illinois has been noted for its illustrious warriors, jurists, and statesmen—Grant, Shields, Logan, Palmer, McClernand, Davis, Trumbull, Breese, Schofield, McAllister, Lincoln, Douglas, Yates, Lovejoy, and countless others, like McDougall and Baker, who won fame in other States; and

Whereas the fame of none of these was more heroically won or more richly deserved than that of one of our deceased citizens, illustrious for historic renown and distinguished for civic service in Europe and America in a new, unexplored field of Christian endeavor, the effect of whose efforts and achievements and the influence of whose spotless life and sublime example has been so marked that the world has wondered and admired the author, the organizer, and advocate of purity and temperance, Illinois's most illustrious deceased citizen, FRANCES E. WILLARD, the uncrowned queen of purity and temperance, whose ashes repose in peace on the shores of Lake Michigan at Evanston, Ill. Her life, like that of her Redeemer, was devoted to the spiritual welfare of mankind, and the world at large has been materially benefited by her prayers and sacrifices. Radiant with a halo of all the virtues, her face shone with the light of intelligence. Her marvelous abilities energized all around and about her, while her gentleness, tact, and self-sacrificing spirit calmed every storm that arose in the councils which were graced and blessed by her presence. Her grand life is a "beacon light" to the good and the true of all sexes, races, and creeds in the civilized world, and her wonderful achievements are lights and landmarks on the cliffs of fame, which will for all time illumine the paths of millions of women wherever civilization has a footing, which is where woman is duly appreciated; and

Whereas the priceless heritage of such a life belongs of right to Illinois; and

Whereas she glories in it and deems it "worthy of national commemoration:" Therefore,

To immortalize it and show to all nations how exalted a sphere woman occupies in this great State, the following law is placed upon our statute books. * * *

The commissioners appointed by Governor Tanner were: Miss Anna A. Gordon, Evanston; Mrs. Susanna M. D. Fry, Evanston; W. R. Jewell, Danville; Mary E. Metzgar, Moline; John J. Mitchell, Chicago.

The commissioners appropriately awarded the fashioning of this statue to an American woman, Helen Farnsworth Mears.

By this act of the State of Illinois through its legislature, the first statue of a woman is to stand in Statuary Hall among other famous Americans who have done sufficiently great work to justify some State of the Union in thus honoring their memory.

Of the population of the United States, there are 37,178,127 females and 38,816,448 males. In the moral and religious work of the world woman is conceded by all to have taken a part and exerted an influence fully commensurate with her proportionate numbers. Yes, I believe her to have been the larger factor in the moral and religious advance of mankind.

In the last half century her intellectual life has rapidly widened with the growth of education and intelligence. In those nations at the present time where is now found the largest measure of political liberty, the highest standard of living, and the greatest individual prosperity and happiness are to be found for woman the greatest civil rights, the largest freedom of action, the widest field of opportunities.

In nearly every State of the Union the restraints of the common law have been removed by legislative action and woman has been given every legal right excepting that of suffrage with well-nigh a universal acquiescence.

In a few States the unrestricted right of suffrage has been accorded her, and in many others the right to vote for school officers has been extended to her.

In no other nation of the world have the political rights of women been broadened as rapidly as they have in this country. Her prominence in the educational work of the United States meets with no denial. Her impress upon the life of the nation has become more and more apparent, and always for good. She has contributed her full share in the achievements of our nation. She has not only molded the character and trained the intellect of our citizenship, but has been a worthy and equal companion with her sons and husband in after life in their private enterprises and their public duties.

If the most distinguished of those who are immortalized in marble in yonder Hall could speak their belief as to the greatest factor in their secured fame, the answer would undoubtedly be, "My mother."

Therefore it seems to me that the decision of my State was a most appropriate and wise one in selecting in this day and age from her illustrious sons and daughters the best known and most universally loved woman in the United States, FRANCES E. WILLARD, as the one to be commemorated in marble and stand in the national Capitol, as an evidence of our appreciation of a singularly beautiful and useful life.

Descended from Puritan stock, with an ancestry especially notable in religious and educational work; born in New York, taken as a child to Ohio, and moving from thence later in the typical prairie schooner to her forest home in Wisconsin, where she spent her girlhood, and finally commencing her young womanhood at Evanston, Ill., and retaining her home there, to be brought back at the time of her death to be buried, she was essentially an American.

Born on September 28, 1839, at Churchville, N. Y., and passing away February 20, 1898, at New York City, she witnessed the development of American civilization from a primitive condition through its development of almost sixty years. The measure of a human life is its motive rather than its accomplishments. Back of the great achievements for the nation accomplished through the guidance of Abraham Lincoln are the motives which moved him, the principles which controlled him.

To-day we have enjoyed the blessings which are the fruition of his work so long that we hardly stop to appreciate them; but the American people still hunger for every stray incident concerning his personal life which in any way aids in the further interpretation of the character of this man, who in the midst of failure would have remained the lover of humanity. [Applause.]

As with Lincoln, the closer one studies the incidents of the life of FRANCES E. WILLARD, the fuller the details of her daily life and its purposes are made known, the more evident it becomes that she was first and foremost of all a lover of humanity, and that the one purpose of her life was to devote it to the best advantage for the uplifting of her kind.

She regarded her life as a "charge to keep," and it is said that she was guided by the spirit of the rocking-chair lullaby sung to her by her father:

> To serve the present age,
>   My calling to fulfill,
> Oh, may it all my powers engage
>   To do my Master's will.

From a lisping child she was nurtured under religious influences and imbued with the thoughts that her life should be devoted to high and noble purposes, and hence after her education had been completed at Northwestern University and she had commenced her life's work further preparation as dean of the Woman's College at Evanston her constant aim was to impress upon her students the importance of a purposeful life.

The oft-repeated question to her girl students was, "What do you intend to do in life?" The great object to her in education was the development of character. "What shall we do with our lives?" was the question ringing through her life as a teacher and reformer. She was proud of her sex. She strove to elevate it. She endeavored to broaden its opportunities, to enlarge its usefulness, to increase its influence, to uplift its purposes. If her life was viewed from the standpoint of her influence upon the women of the United States, without regard to her work elsewhere or upon men, she still would be the greatest figure of our country in woman's work and woman's betterment. [Applause.]

Her educational work gave a distinct impetus to the higher education of women and accident played an important part in taking her from this field into the larger national work for purity and temperance. She displayed wonderful powers of organization and executive ability as head of the National Woman's Christian Temperance Union and as president of

the World's Woman's Christian Temperance Union, the latter
of which she founded. Other women have become distinguished and national figures, but no one of her kind ever
became so universally known and loved throughout the entire
land in the humblest homes. She reached down into the
lives of the millions and made her influence felt, and broadened and sweetened lives and changed their purpose for the
better to the extent, perhaps, that no man or other woman
of America has ever done. [Applause.]

She broadened her culture and enlarged her knowledge of
life by study abroad in Europe and in the East; but all of the
powers of this richly endowed woman were devoted to the single
purpose of her life.

The motto of her order, "For God, and home, and native
land," was manifest in her every effort. She rightly con-
ceived that the homes of America should be the safeguards
of the nation, and hence her philanthropic work was devoted
to the elevation of the home life. Her face is familiar to
almost every child as well as those of maturer years from
ocean to ocean. And what is more important, the principles
for what that face stood are quite as familiar. She addressed
large audiences in every city of 10,000 people and upward
in the United States and in many of smaller population. She
met the test of the orator, for she won converts and changed
lives through the medium of her speeches.

As an orator she ever remained the woman, and throughout
her work her methods were distinctly womanly. Her activity
was simply wonderful, and the energy which she was able to
sustain with her delicate body was a constant surprise to her
friends. She practically had no leisure. And the influence
of the female organizations which were under her chief control
have certainly left a deep and permanent impress upon Ameri-

can life and that of the world. Did she complete the vast
work in which she was engaged? Did she consummate the
complete reformation of the world? Ah, no. It is manifest
from all history that the moral evolution of mankind is most
exceedingly slow. Is to succeed the test of greatness? From
the illustrious men whose figures and memories are perpetuated
in yonder Hall select one whose great work was accomplished
to its full extent ! Not one. The future is full of problems
for the centuries. It is for each man and woman to do his
little part. Be it said, however, that the moral tone of the
people of the United States is higher, the field of woman
enlarged and fuller of hope, and the future of the United
States is brighter for the life of this woman, honored by the
State and nation because her work was good and immortal,
because FRANCES E. WILLARD yet speaks. [Applause.]

Mr. Speaker, I take great pleasure and congratulate my
fellow-citizens of this Republic upon the fact that we place
woman upon a higher standard than is done in any other
civilized nation in the world. [Applause.] The dissemination
of education in the last twenty years has brought about new
ideals concerning the proper elements which make up the successful mother, which enables her to perform all of the duties
connected with the fashioning of human souls, with the building of human character, with the forecasting of the future of
human lives. It is no longer believed in the United States
that a woman is sufficiently informed and equipped if she is
able to do the physical duties connected with the household.
We now understand that she has the most delicate task of all
other occupations. She has the most important task for the
future of the Republic, because this Republic rests for its
safety upon the character of its citizenship. The child is the
father of the man, and it is the women of America who give

direction to the trend of mature life; it is the women who first implant the character of aspirations which afterwards manifest themselves in the active manhood of the United States. So I say, Mr. Speaker, that the State of Illinois is going forward in taking this new step, when she presumes that the women of the United States, with the important duties which they have to perform to society as well as to their families, have a right to a part in this Hall, commemorated to the forms of those who have done great work in the world. [Applause.]

Address of Mr. Littlefield, of Maine

Mr. SPEAKER: By an act of Congress approved July 2, 1864, the President was authorized ''to invite each and all the States to provide and furnish statues in marble or bronze, not exceeding two in number for each State, of deceased persons who have been citizens thereof and illustrious for their historic renown or for distinguished civic or military services.'' The ''old Hall of the House of Representatives'' was set apart ''as a National Statuary Hall'' for the purpose indicated. Thus was established the Valhalla of the Republic. Nineteen States only have thus far placed their candidates for statuary fame therein. Five of these—Illinois, Indiana, Kansas, Maine, and Wisconsin—have but one representative each. The reason for the selection of some of these candidates does not appear to be conspicuously obvious.

The services and historic renown of such men as Roger Sherman, Jonathan Trumbull, O. P. Morton, John J. Ingalls, Samuel Adams, Charles Carroll, William King, Lewis Cass, Thomas H. Benton, Daniel Webster, James A. Garfield, Nathanael Greene, Roger Williams, Samuel Houston, and James Collamore are so well known as to fully justify them in filling a niche in this Hall of Fame.

Some of them contributed in a large degree to the building of the Republic. It is a singular and interesting fact that while the list of our Presidents contains many of the most distinguished men of our history, only one (James A. Garfield, one of the most intellectual of them all) has found a place here. While "military services" is an eligible feature, besides that chivalric old warrior of San Jacinto, Samuel Houston, none of them can be said to have achieved any distinction in the trade of war except the gallant soldier Gen. James Shields, who until to-day has been the sole representative from the State of Illinois. He has the unique distinction of having represented three States in the Senate of the United States. Except as they are so made by this selection, not many of them are or will be "illustrious for their historic renown." It is possible that in many instances the most appropriate selections may not have been made, and that but for these statues some of them would never have emerged from kindly oblivion.

That Illinois has been for some time represented only in part is from no lack of worthy material. She has long had eminent men worthy of this great honor. Some of the most distinguished men of our history, so great and distinguished that they stand out like mountain peaks almost alone in the sky line of historic perspective, belong to Illinois.

No soldier deserves more or will live longer in the hearts of his countrymen for great services rendered, from Washington until now, than the unassuming but indomitable Grant. His fame is Illinois's.

The student of our political history will never read of a more brilliant figure than the little giant of the West, the great war Democrat, the prince of debaters, the patriot, Stephen A. Douglas. [Applause.] In Illinois he lived and died.

The greatest figure in American history — yes, one of the greatest figures in the history of the world — the immortal, celestial, martyred Lincoln, belongs alike to Illinois. She has many other illustrious sons. With all this wealth of material Illinois to-day places in this great Pantheon the statue of a beautiful Christian woman, who has a deserved and world-wide renown for "distinguished civic" services.

By her own efforts she had "achieved greatness." Without this legislative recognition her name and fame were secure. It was written on the fleshly tablets of millions of human hearts beyond all power of effacement. The beautiful marble, the enduring bronze, or the eternal granite were not necessary to perpetuate it. It was as firmly fixed "as though graven with an iron pen and lead in the rock forever."

This is the first time that our Valhalla has been graced, adorned, and honored by the statue of a woman. FRANCES ELIZABETH WILLARD can fittingly and appropriately represent her sex in this distinguished and honorable company. Illinois honors herself by giving to womankind this noble recognition. It is a most gratifying reflection that if the mighty and sainted shade of the departed Lincoln could have been consulted it would have no doubt concurred with hearty enthusiasm in this selection. She was the especial representative of a great cause in whose principles he religiously believed and whose tenets he faithfully practiced. Abraham Lincoln was a total abstainer. The sincerity of his habits and practice in this regard were subjected to the highest test when the committee to notify him of his nomination as a candidate of the Republican party for the Presidency visited him at his modest home in Springfield.

After having received the momentous message, in the presence of that distinguished and notable gathering he said:

Gentlemen, we must pledge our mutual health in the most healthy beverage which God has given to man. It is the only beverage I have ever used or allowed in my family, and I can not conscientiously depart from it now on this occasion. It is pure Adam's ale.

In a private and confidential letter written June 11, 1860, in referring to this incident, he wrote:

Having kept house sixteen years and having never held the "cup" to the lips of my friends then, my judgment was that I should not, in my new position, change my habits in this respect.

How the moral courage and absolute sincerity of the man is exemplified by this incident! While he did not make his views offensively conspicuous, he did not hesitate when occasion called to avow them.

Hon. Lawrence Weldon, of Washington, D. C., a distinguished and able judge of the Court of Claims, traveled from his home to Bloomington, Ill., on September 12, 1854, for the purpose of hearing Judge Douglas discuss the political issues of the day. At that time he had never met Mr. Lincoln, who was in town attending court. Mr. Weldon was present in Douglas's room at the hotel when Douglas declined an invitation to divide the time with Mr. Lincoln.

On a sideboard were liquors of various kinds. Lincoln came in and Douglas introduced him to Mr. Weldon. Social drinking was then a well-nigh universal custom, and in a few minutes Douglas said: "Mr. Lincoln, won't you have something to drink?" To this Mr. Lincoln replied: "No, Judge, I think not." "What," said Douglas, "do you belong to the temperance society?" "No," rejoined Mr. Lincoln, "I don't belong to any temperance society, but I am temperate in this, to wit: I don't drink anything." This incident I have from the Judge's lips.

Nor did he hesitate to preach in accordance with his practice.

On Washington's Birthday, February 22, 1842, in his own home city, he delivered one of the most remarkable temperance addresses extant. Referring to the drink habit, he said:

Let us make it as unfashionable to withhold our names from the temperance pledge as for husbands to wear their wives' bonnets to church, and instances will be just as rare in the one case as in the other.

Speaking of the dignity and vital importance of the temperance reform, he said:

If the relative grandeur of revolutions shall be estimated by the great amount of human misery they alleviate and the small amount they inflict, then indeed will this be the grandest the world shall have ever seen. Of our political revolution of "'76" we all are justly proud. It has given us a degree of political freedom far exceeding that of any other of the nations on the earth. In it the Old World has found a solution of that long-mooted problem as to the capability of man to govern himself.

In it was the germ which has vegetated and still is to grow and expand into the universal liberty of mankind. But with all these glorious results, past, present, and to come, it had its evils too. It breathed forth famine, swam in blood, and rode on fire, and long, long after the orphan's cry and widow's wail continued to break the sad silence that ensued. These were the price, the inevitable price, paid for the blessings it brought.

Turn now to the temperance revolution. In it we shall find a stronger bondage broken, a viler slavery manumitted, a greater tyrant deposed. In it more of want supplied, more disease healed, more sorrow assuaged. By it no orphans starving, no widows weeping. By it none wounded in feeling, none injured in interest.

And what a noble ally is this to the cause of political freedom. With such an aid its march can not fail to be on and on until every son on earth shall drink in rich fruition the sorrow-quenching draft of perfect liberty. Happy day, when all appetite is controlled, all passions subdued, all manners subjected, mind—all-conquering mind—shall live and move, the monarch of the world. Glorious consummation! "Hail, fall of Fury! Reign of Reason, hail!" This rings with no uncertain sound.

The momentous character of this great question never was and probably never will be stated more forcibly, vigorously effectively, and truthfully. He was a most vigorous and effective advocate of that logical corollary of total abstinence for the individual, prohibition for the State. He spent weeks in Illinois campaigning for the adoption of the Maine law in that State. The following excerpts were the keynotes of his speeches:

This legalized liquor traffic, as carried on in the saloons and grogshops, is the great tragedy of civilization. The saloon has proved itself to be the greatest foe, the most blighting curse that has ever found a home in our modern civilization, and this is the reason why I am a political Prohibitionist. Prohibition brings the desired result. It suppresses the saloon by law. It stamps and brands the saloonkeeper as a criminal in the sight of God and man. * * *

By licensing the saloon we feed with one hand the fires of appetite we are striving to quench with the other. While this state of things continues let us know that this war is all our own—both sides of it—until this guilty connivance of our own actions shall be withdrawn. I am a Prohibitionist because prohibition destroys destruction.

In 1863 he declared that—

The reasonable man of the world has long since agreed that intemperance is one of the greatest, if not the greatest, of all evils among mankind.

That his wide and varied experience never changed his earlier views is clear from the statement made by him to Mr. Mervin on the very morning of his assassination:

After reconstruction, the next great work before us is the probibition of the liquor traffic in all of the States and Territories.

Inspired by this high and lofty purpose he entered the presence of his Maker.

Abraham Lincoln was neither a crank, a fanatic, a hairbrained enthusiast, nor a hypocrite. None of us need be ashamed to follow where he nobly led. [Applause.] His footsteps have made it holy ground. If the shades of the departed revisit the haunts of men, we may feel assured that he would behold with the greatest of satisfaction the recognition of the cause in which he believed with his whole heart by the erection of this memorial to the memory of this brilliant and devoted woman.

This statue in our Valhalla is a fit and merited recognition of all that is highest, noblest, and best in womanhood.

In the evolution and development of the race from barbarism to Christian civilization woman has been gradually emancipated from the subordinate and servile position to which the aboriginal savage, at a period dominated by physical force and unfeeling, ignorant brutality, had arbitrarily relegated her. While her emancipation is not yet complete, it has been tardily keeping pace with our developing civilization and is in no small degree the indication of that development. She is now no longer "something better than his dog, a little dearer than his horse."

She is not only the equal, but, in many respects, immeasurably the superior of the lords of creation. Still, in some respects before the law, with its many relics and survivals of the dark ages, she still wears the badge of inferiority. These Miss WILLARD struggled manfully to remove. Notwithstanding the arbitrary disadvantages under which she has labored, women have in all ages given us shining examples of greatness and genius that need not shrink from comparison with the sterner sex.

Sappho, it is conceded, has never been surpassed in sweetness and grace by any lyric poet, ancient or modern. Plato called her the "tenth muse," and Aristotle ranked her with Homer. Socrates sat at the feet of Aspasia and learned philosophy. She taught Pericles statesmanship, and is said to have written some of his most famous orations. The modest, pure, guileless girl of 17—Joan of Arc—took the command of an army and led it to victory with a success that makes the fame and supernatural genius of the great Napoleon pale their "ineffectual fires." It has been well said "she is easily and by far the most extraordinary person the human race has ever produced."

The enlightened enterprise and lofty public spirit of Isabella of Spain made it possible for Columbus to discover the New World, which was destined to become the home of the mightiest republic the world ever saw.

St. Theresa was canonized by the Pope for the great reforms she wrought in Catholic orders, and the value of her religious writings.

Queen Elizabeth, although crafty and cruel, was learned and able, and the Elizabethan period is one of the most splendid in English history.

Enlightened beyond her time, the Empress Maria Theresa abolished torture and the inquisition, and was one of the greatest of the Austrian rulers.

Catherine of Russia was the patron of learning, and ruled with a truly masculine vigor.

Profound in moral and political philosophy, unequaled in dialectic discussion, Madame de Staël had the proud distinction of compelling the haughty and intolerant Napoleon to banish her twice through fear of her pen that was "mightier than the sword."

Abigail Adams was one of the incomparable mothers of the Revolution, whose letters to her son are uplifting and ennobling, and still the highest guide to right living.

Queen Louisa of Prussia, the noble and good, was the mother of kingly kings. Elizabeth Barrett Browning was easily among the first of modern poets. George Eliot was the Shakespeare of women, a novelist of the highest order. The world-renowned philanthropist, the John Howard of her sex, was found in Florence Nightingale. Rachel, the magnificent, reached the highest altitude of dramatic expression. In Jenny Lind the human voice in song found its most popular and attractive expression. In the professor's study in beautiful Brunswick, within the shade of Bowdoin's classic walls, the philippic was written that was the most powerful factor in precipitating the fratricidal struggle that was not to end until human slavery was no more.

After Harriet Beecher Stowe's Uncle Tom's Cabin and the Dred Scott decision no human power could avert the crisis. And when the struggle came this stanza—

> In the beauty of the lilies Christ was born across the sea,
> With a glory in His bosom that transfigures you and me;
> As He died to make men holy, let us die to make men free,
> While God is marching on—

of Julia Ward Howe inspired the courage, sustained the valor, renewed the patriotic fervor, and steeled the arm of the battling hosts of freemen.

To such as these we can well bow down and worship. They are the splendid creations of a great race.

In this brilliant galaxy of great women FRANCES ELIZABETH WILLARD has placed her name. Her deeds have written it there. Educated, cultured, refined, journalist, author, and professor, she abandoned them all that she might devote her life to the advancement and promotion of the cause that was near and dear to her, the sacred cause that has the soul-inspiring watchword, "For God and home and native land."

Whittier beautifully and appropriately says, in lines addressed to her:

> She knew the power of banded ill,
> But felt that love was stronger still,
> And organized, for doing good,
> The world's united womanhood.

She deliberately relinquished the brilliant position of dean of the first woman's college connected with a university in America to go out penniless, alone, and unheralded, because her spirit had caught the rhythm of the women's footsteps as they bridged the distance between the home and the saloon in the pentecostal days of the temperance crusade. She relinquished that which women hold dearest and most sacred, the shelter of home.

It was that other women might, under their own "vine and fig tree," enjoy the blessings of a pure and virtuous home that she sacrificed and toiled and endured. She found the Woman's Christian Temperance Union a national organization. She made it international. Its labors were confined to one country; she made its activities 'world wide. Its motto of "For God and home and native land," with divinely inspired evangel hope and faith, she transformed to "For God and home and every land."

In 1883 she became the president of this organization, based upon "personal purity of life, including total abstinence from all narcotic poisons, the protection of the home by outlawing the traffic in intoxicating liquors, opium, tobacco, and the suppression by law of gambling and Sunday desecration; the enfranchisement of the women of all nations; and the establishment of courts of national and international arbitration which shall banish war from the world."

Before her untimely death she had the infinite satisfaction of knowing that it was firmly planted in fifty different countries, where, in the common language of the heart, though in many different tongues, it "ministered to all good and true women who are willing to clasp hands in one common effort to protect their homes and loved ones from the ravages of drink," by "an organization without a pattern save that seen in heavenly vision upon the mount of faith, and without a peer among the sisterhoods that have grouped themselves around the cross of Christ." Millions were brought within the reach of its elevating, humanizing, Christianizing influences. These gentle persuasive ministrations proceeded in the faith that "the banner and the sword were never yet the symbol of man's grandest victories," and that the time was at hand "to listen to the voice of that inspired philosophy which through all ages has been gently saying, 'The race is not to the swift nor the battle to the strong.'"

While she had extraordinary executive and administrative ability, she could not have accomplished her great work had she not been divinely blessed with qualities and graces of the mind, heart, and person that are seldom found combined.

Attractive, engaging, and beautiful in person, with a musical voice of marvelous sweetness and purity, intellectual, logical, persuasive, and eloquent, she had a platform presence and manner that made her easily one of the most eloquent and effective of orators.

If true eloquence is to be measured by the effect produced upon the hearers, she had few equals and no superiors.

No repetition of her language can reproduce the charm that clothed it as it fell from her lips. She brought all the wealth of culture and learning to her work. That she realized the importance of the highest ideals in literature and keenly appreciated the infinite harm of covering vice with an attractive garb and minimizing its wickedness and infamy, was vividly portrayed by her address on the presentation of the portrait of Mrs. Hayes. She then said:

What shall be said of the wizard pen of the romancer, with its boundless sweep through time and space? Alas, with what borrowed livery of the imagination has it not disguised the dangers of the moderate drinker and bedecked the brutal pleasures of the debauchee. Heroes have been men mighty to drink wine, and heroines have found their prototype in Hebe, cupbearer to the gods. From the sensuous pages of the Greek romancers, through mediæval tale and legend, the reeling pages of Fielding, the chivalric pageantry of Scott, the splendid society drama of Thackeray, and the matchless character panoramas of Dickens, down to our own society novels; in all the witching volumes over which the beaming eyes of youth have lingered the high lights of convivial enjoyment have been brought out in most vivid word painting, and its black shadows as studiously concealed. Now be it remembered that the poet, the artist, and the novelist—mighty interpreters of nature and the soul—will always maintain their empire over the human heart so long as it is a willing captive to the love of beauty and the beauty of love. So that until we win an assured place for the temperance reform in these supremely influential realms of thought and expression our success can not be considered as permanent. Until genius, with her starry eyes, shall be gently persuaded to lay her choicest trophies at the feet of temperance there will remain for us much territory to be possessed.

The most striking and unique incident of her work was the celebrated Polyglot Petition for Home Protection presented "to the governments of the world." It was signed throughout the civilized world, and in fifty different languages. The signatures mounted upon canvas, four columns abreast, made more than a mile of canvas and nearly 5 miles of solid signatures, 771,200 in all. It represented by societies and associations over 7,500,000 persons. It was ten years in circulation. In an eloquent and impressive speech, Miss WILLARD presented it to President Cleveland February 19, 1895. The English branch was headed by Lady Henry Somerset, the magnificent English woman who is leading in temperance reform in England. On the American petition, like Abou Ben Adhem, and for the same reason, Neal Dow's name "led all the rest."

More than fifty years ago General Dow, at the request of the broken-hearted wife of a drunken husband, called upon a saloon keeper and urged him not to sell to the unfortunate man. He was ordered out of the saloon with the remark, "There's my license on the wall. This man is one of my best customers. I'll not offend him." "Do you mean that you will go right on selling whisky to him?" said Dow. "I shall sell to him just as long as he can pay for his drinks,"

replied the saloon keeper. As General Dow left the saloon
he said, "The people of the State of Maine will see how long
you will go on selling." In 1851 came the Maine law. With
the exception of two years—1856–1858—it has been steadfastly
adhered to ever since, though not as continuously and effectively enforced as it ought to be. It has been estimated from
actual sales taken from old account books that prior to 1851
the people of Raymond, then a small town of 1,149 souls,
with a valuation of about $150,000, consumed more liquor
in every period of eighteen years than the entire valuation of
the town. To-day no liquor tax is paid in the town, and
while its population has decreased to 823, its valuation has
increased to $213,576. The soil and climate of Maine are
not such as make the development and accumulation of wealth
an easy task. The natural facilities that contribute to that
end are much inferior to those found in the Middle States,
the South, and the great West.

Nature has done little for her beyond furnishing the opportunity for the development of an energetic, enterprising, vigorous, hardy, intelligent, and sturdy people. They have sent
thousands upon thousands of their hard-earned savings during
the last two decades into the far West, attracted by the expec-
tation of a profitable return thereon. Very few of these thousands ever have returned, or ever will return, thus diminishing
her savings and impairing her wealth.

There is nothing in her policy or law that differentiates her
from her sister States except the prohibitory law. The only
reliable indicator of the thrift and prosperity of a people is its
savings. In this respect the people of Maine, fostered by legislation that preserves their earnings, challenges all comparison.

In 1850 she had no savings banks; in 1900 she had deposited
$66,132,677 in her savings banks. While she ranks only thir-

teenth in population among the States of the Union, there are only six that outrank her in the amount of savings deposits, and only seven which have a larger number of depositors.

Illinois, with about seven times the population of Maine, has $7,000,000 less savings deposit. Ohio, with nearly six times the population of Maine, has $22,000,000 less deposits. Pennsylvania, with nine times the population of Maine, has only $40,000,000 more deposits. In other words, Maine has in her savings banks $95.22 for every inhabitant. Illinois has only $13.43; Ohio, $10.71; and Pennsylvania, $16.12. While Maine's population has increased since 1850 only 20 per cent, her valuation per capita has increased 252 per cent. A single concrete, unimpeachable, significant fact like this, bearing living witness to the efficacy of her settled policy, is of more value than reams of newspaper columns full of ill-considered and unfounded assertions that the law has been a practical failure. [Applause.] It is entirely true, as eloquently and incisively declared by Governor Cobb, of Maine, in his recent noble message, that this law "lies very close to the heart and conscience of thousands of the men and women" of Maine.

Miss WILLARD believed in the wisdom and efficacy of this legislation. Sincere and zealous enthusiast as she was, she was essentially and always broad minded, catholic, and tolerant in her views. She knew that intelligent discussion and free and open agitation would in the end disclose and firmly establish the truth. In her last important public utterance she laid down Cobden's rule as her guide: "Never assume that the motives of the man who is opposed to you in policy or argument are one whit less pure and disinterested than your own." Commenting, she said:

But, alas, it is our custom to consider that wisdom will die with us, and that truthfulness first had its being when we were born. While the facts

are, speaking broadly, that being subject to a certain pressure of education certain great masses of men look upon them in another way, and
nothing short of that argumentation which politics furnishes will enable
both groups to reach at last an equilibrium of thought by leavening the
entire lump with two different kinds of education, so that one view shall
modify the other.   And the greatest of all these is charity.

The home is the basic unit of our Christian civilization.
It is the foundation stone upon which our free institutions
rest.   Upon its integrity, purity, and character the character
and quality of our civilization depend.   It is a holy shrine.
Whatever profanes it pollutes the sacred temple of liberty
itself.   Whoever defends and ennobles it insures to our
children and our children's children the blessings of freedom
and the enduring of a "government of the people, for the
people, and by the people."   A civilization based upon a
lecherous and debauched home is rotten at the core.

Statesmen, warriors, and patriots may strive and build and
achieve, but all their striving, building, and achieving is in
vain, even "as sounding brass, or a tinkling cymbal," if it
djsregards the eternal moral verities and does not conserve
the true happiness and the highest welfare of mankind.   This
divinely gifted woman bent every energy, shaped every purpose, and devoted every aspiration of a godly life to the
consummation of this happiness and welfare.   It is meet that
her work should be thus recognized.

This statue stands, and always will stand, as the highest
and truest embodiment of all that is noblest, best, and divinest
in the womanhood of America and the enduring memorial of
"whatever things are of good report" in our Christian civilization.   [Great applause.]

Address of Mr. Rainey, of Illinois

Mr. SPEAKER: Forty-one years ago, when the two great sections of our country still contended in awful battle, Congress passed an act making out of the old Hall of the House of Representatives a national gallery, to which each State was invited to contribute the statues of two of her most famous citizens. Since then the States have been responding until now nineteen of them are represented here.

In this Hall of Fame statues of warriors and of statesmen stand side by side.

Men acquire fame upon the battlefield, amid the pomp and glory of war. This opportunity is denied to women. Men acquire fame as diplomats and statesmen, but this opportunity also is closed to women; and so we have in Statuary Hall figures of heroic size presented by the States; nearly all of them are the portraits in stone and marble and bronze of men who have had access to these great fields of human effort and human ambition; for them the door of opportunity stood always open.

Until to-day no State has contributed the statue of a woman. No one imagined forty-one years ago, when this act was passed, that the heroic figure of a woman would ever stand beneath that Dome. But the world is growing in more ways than one; and the world is ready now to believe that a courageous womanly woman makes as heroic a figure as a brave manly man. [Applause.]

When the act was passed which established this Hall of Fame men were winning the right to a place here upon the field of battle at the head of crushing squadrons of cavalry, or directing the movement of long lines of infantry, amid the roar of cannon and all the din of war. Their statues—some of them—are already here, and there are more to come. But the real battle which made this a nation, one and indivisible, was fought and won after the surrender at Appomatox; after the men of the blue army had returned to their Northern homes; after the men of the gray army had sadly gone back to ruined plantations throughout the pleasant Southland. The real victory was won long after the green grass was growing and and the flowers were blooming upon the graves of the men who fell in this, the greatest civil war the world ever saw. It was a victory won in a battle waged by men and women of the South, standing shoulder to shoulder with men and women of the North—a peaceful struggle to quench the fires of sectional hate and antagonism.

It was at this time that there came out of the North a new leader—not a leader of armed men, but a leader of unarmed women—a woman of supreme capacity, mental and moral and physical. Illinois to-day presents her statue, exquisitely carved out of the whitest of Carrara marble, to the nation as her contribution to this great Hall of Fame. [Applause.]

In the years which followed the war one of the forces most potent to sweep away the mists and let in the sunlight upon North and South alike was the army of women, led by FRANCES E. WILLARD, marching through the North and the South following the white banners upon which she had inscribed the motto, "For God and home and native land." In the dark days which followed the war she furnished the common ground upon which all could stand, whether they lived under bright skies where the magnolia blooms or under grayer skies in the colder North.

She led the fight for the home, for personal purity, for better habits of living, for the rights of children, for the uplifting of women. Upon these great subjects she delivered addresses in almost all the towns and cities of the country containing a population of 5,000 and upward. On one of her campaigns she traveled 30,000 miles, speaking almost every day in crowded halls and churches.

With chains of gold stretching across the gulf which divided the sections she bound together the homes of the North and the homes of the South until the dividing chasm disappeared and a mighty nation moves forward under one banner with resistless force to the tremendous destiny prepared for it by the omnipotent God. If peace hath its victories, it is peculiarly appropriate that Miss WILLARD'S statue should stand here under this Dome. In the State which produced a Lincoln, a Douglas, and a Logan we consider her one of our greatest citizens. [Applause.]

The past century has been called the woman's century. During the latter half of the century a woman sat on the throne of England, and under her gentle and wise influence literature and the arts flourished, and the commerce of the English nation whitened every sea. During the same period of time the woman we honor here to-day, with gentle strength was fighting for the success of all the higher moral forces. She made her opportunities—none of them were inherited. She did not come into a throne by divine right; but her purity of purpose, her loyalty at all times, her tenderness, her breadth of human sympathy, her resistless energy, won for her the title of "the uncrowned queen," and in the hearts of five million true women of the land she reigned supreme.

Three hundred years ago, on the banks of a beautiful river in far-away India, at fabulous cost a king erected a tomb in memory of a woman. With towering minarets of whitest marble it stands to-day the most splendid building ever erected by man. The women of America have erected in memory of FRANCES E. WILLARD a monument not made of marble, which crumbles with the passing centuries, but made of that enduring material which withstands the ravages of time—a monument of human love and human admiration and human sympathy. [Applause.]

She was a true child of the prairie. During the fifty years of her active career she lived in the State of Illinois, and from her modest, quiet cottage in the village of Evanston, where only the murmurs of the great lake broke the stillness, she issued forth, a modern Joan of Arc, to fight the nation's enemies—aglow with purpose—wearing the armor of truth and womanly purity. She has won a place in the temple of the truly great. FRANCES E. WILLARD is dead, her soul has gone beyond the stars, but her memory lives.

The State of Illinois—always the home of great men—mindful of the fact that she is entitled to no more places in this Hall, presents now to the nation the statue of this woman, cunningly carved, by a woman, out of the finest and the whitest of marble. [Long-continued applause.] ·

Address of Mr. Brooks, of Colorado

Mr. SPEAKER: Colorado owes much to Illinois. From her
we derived our form of State constitution; from her also we
took many of our statute laws; from her came many of the
pioneers who helped to give form and shape to the State's
new life; but no debt of Colorado to her mother State exceeds
in importance that which she owes for the precious gift of
memory of the life and character of FRANCES E. WILLARD.
Herself one of the nation's empire builders, she appeals with
peculiar force to the thousands of noble, constructive men and
women who look to such examples for their guidance and for
their support.

Miss WILLARD was unusually adapted to meet such needs.
She had in her own life seen and been a part of the growth
and development of two of our great Commonwealths. She
had played a most important part in directing and ennobling
the life of those communities before she entered upon her
larger and more enduring labors. The men and women of
Colorado who are trying to reproduce in the mountain surroundings of that State the ideas and ideals for which she
gave her whole life's devotion find at every step abundant
material in her history to serve as their own model and to her
they look for leadership.

Her life has not been without its definite, tangible, present
results in that State at least. Much that she labored for has
there been achieved. Colorado is one of the four States of
the Union which have accorded to woman full civic rights,

which recognize in fullest measure her equality before the law, and place her on a plane in all respects equal to that occupied by her brothers. It has been a successful experiment, and the people everywhere give it a full measure of approval. In every line of civic activities that community has received and has appreciated the benefit of woman's counsels, help, and active constructive work; and these counsels and that help have had a most stimulating effect in every phase of life.

In none of Colorado's institutions for higher education, save the technical school of mining engineering, is any line of sex distinction drawn. Yearly these institutions are not only more and more adding distinction and bringing honor to our State, but they are approaching more and more the ideals of the woman who was not only a great reformer, philanthropist, and religious worker, but a great, positive force in the educational world.

Of the seven Members of this House who have been sent here in part by women's votes, three are from the Centennial State. It is therefore proper that I should, on behalf of that State and its noble women, add my voice to the volume of tribute to the life of her whose statue now holds this highly honored position.

In her life she graced and adorned every circle. She added strength and force to every council. She promoted and advanced every good cause to a degree that we do not yet fully appreciate. Others have recounted in glowing terms the features of her life, and have told what she did for civilization and humanity. I do not care to attempt to add anything to what has been said along these lines. Miss WILLARD stands now as a type of the loftiest endeavor of the later years of the nineteenth century. Such a life and such a work knows no sex. It is for mankind.

To-day the nation joins in welcoming this newest addition to our Hall of Fame. It recognizes and pays glad tribute to her intellectual ability, her self-sacrificing work for her race, and the grandeur of her moral worth. It takes her into full fellowship with her heroes of war and peace, her great lawmakers and administrators, as one of those who have done great things for their native land.

The State whose advent into the sisterhood of States marked the opening of the second century of the nation's life can not and will not be unheard among those who at this time are giving utterance to the universal regard for her who is the cause and occasion of these exercises. Not only here, but in the lives and homes of her people she will perpetuate and cherish her memory and strive to emulate and follow her example.

Illinois, the home of her mature life and the scene of her greatest work, has given her an undying fame in the beautiful marble which now graces our halls. The nation has accepted the gift of that marble to cherish and protect. It is for Colorado, with the other States, to secure for her a monument more lasting than bronze, which is to be erected in the loving hearts of the thousands whose lives she has ennobled and uplifted.

The SPEAKER pro tempore (Mr. Mann). The question is on agreeing to the resolution.

The question was taken, and the resolution was unanimously agreed to.

Mr. Foss. Mr. Speaker, I move that the House do now adjourn.

The motion was agreed to; and accordingly (at 5 o'clock and 48 minutes p. m.) the House adjourned to meet to-morrow at 12 o'clock noon.

O